Royal Air Force
In Germany
1945-1993

Royal Air Force Historical Society Seminar held jointly with
Defence Studies (RAF) at The Joint Services Command and
Staff College, Bracknell on 9 December 1998

The opinions expressed in this publication are those of the contributors concerned and are not necessarily those held by the Royal Air Force Historical Society.

Copyright © 1999 Royal Air Force Historical Society

First published in the UK in 1999 by the
Royal Air Force Historical Society

British Library Cataloguing in Publication Data available

ISBN 0 9519824 9 4

Typeset and printed in Great Britain by Fotodirect Ltd, Brighton

Royal Air Force Historical Society

Contents

	Page
Welcome by Society Chairman - AVM Baldwin	8
Introduction by ACM Sir Andrew Wilson	9
Historical Background by Gp Capt Taylor	10
A Continental Commitment by Gp Capt Peach	17

Defensive Operations

The Principles of Air Defence by ACM Sir Roger Palin	34
Defensive Operations by AM Macfadyen	44
Ground based Air Defence by Wg Cdr Evans	50
Morning Discussion	58

Offensive Operations

An Operations Overview by Sir Andrew Wilson	63
Strike Operations by Air Cdre Wilkinson	68
Attack Operations by Air Cdre White	83
Reconnaissance by Air Cdre Pitchfork	90
Special Operations - Intelligence by Gp Capt Killick	97
Afternoon Discussion	100

| The Early Years in a Global Context   by Dr Goulter | 105 |
| Historical Perspective   by Sebastian Cox | 111 |

| Final Discussion | 118 |

| Closing Address | 123 |

Selected Abbreviations

1 (BR) Corps	First British Corps (BAOR under NATO).
2TAF	Second Tactical Air Force (ie RAF).
2ATAF	Second Allied Tactical Air Force.
4ATAF	Fourth Allied Tactical Air Force.
AAFCE	Allied Air Forces Central Europe.
AAM	Air-to-Air Missile.
ACE	Allied Command Europe.
ACOC	Air Command Operations Centre.
ADIZ	Air Defence Identification Zone.
AFCENT	Allied Forces Central Europe.
AI	Air Interdiction.
ALARM	Air-Launched Anti-Radiation Missile.
APC	Armament Practice Camp.
ARRC	Allied Rapid Reaction Corps.
ASOC	Air Support Operations Centre.
ATOC	Air Tactical Operations Centre.
AWACS	Airborne Warning and Control System.
BAFO	British Air Forces of Occupation.
BAI	Battlefield Air Interdiction.
BASC	Berlin Air Safety Centre.
BRIXMIS	British Commanders-in-Chiefs' Mission to the Commanders of the Soviet Forces in Germany.
CAP	Combat Air Patrol.
CAS	Close Air Support.
CBU	Cluster Bomb Unit.
CENTAG	Central Army Group.
CEP	Circular Error of Probability.
CIO	Command Intelligence Officer.
COMARRC	Commander Allied Rapid Reaction Corps.
COMSOCONE	Commander Sector Operations Centre One.
COMTWOATAF	Commander, Second Allied Tactical Air Force.
CRC	Control and Reporting Centre.
DIS	Defence Intelligence Staff.
FRA	First Run Attack.
FRG	Federal Republic of Germany.
GDR	German Democratic Republic.
GSFG	Group of Soviet Forces in Germany.

HAS	Hardened Aircraft Shelter.
HIDACZ	High Density Airspace Control Zone.
HIMEZ	High-level Missile Engagement Zone.
INF	Intermediate (Range) Nuclear Forces.
JHQ	Joint Headquarters.
JTF	Joint Task Force.
LABS	Low Altitude Bombing System.
LGB	Laser Guided Bomb.
LTC	Long Term Costings.
MAXEVAL	A station-sponsored major exercise in preparation for a formal TACEVAL (often complemented by smaller scale MINEVALs).
MDAP	Mutual Defence Aid Pact.
MEZ	Missile Engagement Zone.
NATINADS	NATO Integrated Air Defence System.
NORTHAG	Northern Army Group.
OAS	Offensive Air Support.
OCA	Offensive Counter Air.
OLF	Operational Low Flying.
OP	Observation Post.
ORBAT	Order of Battle.
PGM	Precision Guided Munitions.
QRA	Quick Reaction Alert.
SACEUR	Supreme Allied Commander, Europe.
SAM	Surface-to-air Missile.
SHAPE	Supreme Headquarters Allied Powers in Europe.
SHORAD	Short Range Air Defence.
SUPPLAN	The detailed arrangements for a specific aspect of a NATO commander's responsibilities, each plan being identified by a standard alphabetical code, eg a SUPPLAN ALFA covered his nuclear operations and a MIKE his airspace management procedures.
TAA	(Soviet) Tactical Air Army.
TACEVAL	Tactical Evaluation – a NATO-sponsored assessment of a unit's wartime efficiency.
TFR	Terrain Following Radar.
UAV	Unmanned Air Vehicles.
UE	Unit Establishment.
USAFE	United States Air Forces in Europe.
WP	Warsaw Pact.

This map covers the RAF's half-a-century in Germany; it does not relate to any specific date. It shows the broad division of airspace and the locations of HQs, airfields and other facilities used by the RAF from time-to-time.

1   Sylt
2   Schleswigland
3   Jever
4   Oldenburg
5   Ahlhorn
6   Finkenwerder
7   Lübeck
8   Gatow
9   Havelsee
10 Fassberg
11 Celle
12 Wunstorf
13 Bückeburg
14 Bad Eilsen
    (HQ BAFO & 2nd TAF)
15 Nordhorn Range
16 Gütersloh
17 Laarbruch
18 Brüggen
19 Wildenrath
20 Rheindahlen
    (HQ RAFG & 2ATAF)
21 Wegberg Hospital
22 Geilenkirchen
23 Wahn

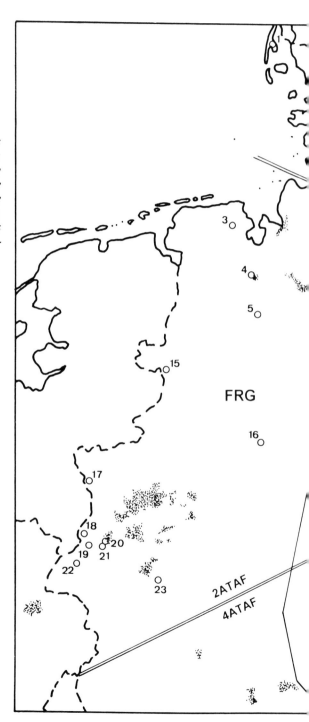

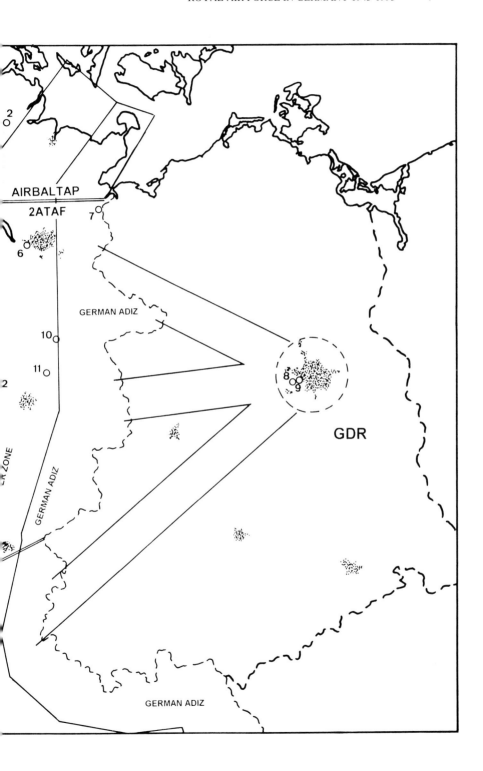

2

AIRBALTAP

2ATAF

7

6

GERMAN ADIZ

10

11

2

GDR

GERMAN ADIZ

8
9

GERMAN ADIZ

Welcome by the Chairman of the Royal Air Force Historical Society

Air Vice-Marshal Nigel Baldwin CB CBE

On behalf of the Society let me thank the Commandant and Air Commodore White for helping us mount this seminar today. In its 12 year history, the Society has held some of its most successful ventures here at Bracknell with all that that has meant for bringing together those who made our history and those who would gain by studying it. With the demise of the RAF Staff College, we, in the Society, have held our breath while the dust has settled hoping that we would, one day, be allowed back in. So long may such arrangements as today continue. It is a real pleasure for those of us who have retired to be back on what is still, in our hearts, an RAF station, but particularly to be amongst a younger generation in uniform.

Air Chief Marshal Sir Andrew 'Sandy' Wilson has masterminded todays' programme ably assisted by Gp Capt Stuart Peach – the RAF's Director of Defence Studies. I and my Committee are very grateful to them – in a voluntary Society such as ours, such enthusiasts are key to any success we may have not just for an event such as today but in also producing eventually, alongside my small editorial team, the written record which, of course, will go to members all over the world.

Sir 'Sandy' knows a bit about RAF Germany. he had six tours there flying Hunters, Phantoms, and Jaguars in the tactical fighter recce role – all on 2 Sqn, eventually as the Squadron Commander. And two tours on the staff of the Headquarters at Rheindahlen firstly as ADC to the C-in-C (the now Marshal of the Royal Air Force Sir Denis Spotswood who we are delighted to see here today) and then, 23 years later, as the Commander-in-Chief himself. Indeed the last C-in-C before the Command was disbanded in 1993.

Sir Sandy, it is a pleasure for me to ask you to chair today.

Introduction by Seminar Chairman

Air Chief Marshal Sir Andrew Wilson KCB AFC

First may I, as your Chairman for the day, add my own very warm welcome. It is a great pleasure to be back at Bracknell amongst so many old friends and, of course, to have the young blood of the Advanced Staff Course with us. Whilst this is clearly not the Bracknell most of us remember it is amazing to see what you get these days for £12m!

I am sharing the platform with four fellow members from No 63 Course. 25 years may seem a long time but in many ways it seems only yesterday. When we arrived here the Commandant of the day, Alisdair Steadman, made a point of telling us all that we should enjoy ourselves as the previous course had had rather a miserable time. At my farewell interview he made the point of telling me that he thought that I had taken his word rather too literally!

Today we review the history of the Royal Air Force in Germany from the end of the Second World War in 1945 to 1993 when I had the sad task of closing down the RAF's last overseas Command. This 48 year period covers a significant time in European history, centred of course on the Cold War, beginning with the Berlin Airlift and ending with the breaching of the Berlin Wall and the subsequent reunification of Germany.

As such it is by far the longest period of RAF history ever reviewed by the Historical Society. We did give thought to restricting our attention to RAF Germany only, since the Command was not formed until 1959 but decided that from a historical point of view, we would have left out perhaps the most significant part – namely the transition from 2TAF through BAFO – which is so essential to a proper understanding of what was the front line of the RAF for nearly 50 years.

Against this background you will appreciate that setting today's agenda has not been an easy exercise. On the one hand we clearly had to cover the ground, and on the other, we wanted to have the main focus on operational matters. Whilst some might have reservations about reviewing such recent history I believe this must be balanced against the advantages of talking about events and issues that are still very much in the corporate memory. And I am happy to note that we have representatives from almost every era in the audience today.

1. Historical Background

Group Captain W J Taylor OBE

Bill Taylor joined the RAF as a technician in 1967 and was a sergeant by the time he was commissioned into the Engineer Branch in 1973. Since then his appointments have included Brüggen (Jaguars), 27Sqn (Tornados) and OC Engineering and Supply Wing to the Bloodhound force as a Wg Cdr during 1987-90. He is currently stationed at Innsworth where he is the Logistics and Contracts Manager within the Training Group Defence Agency.

He holds a private pilots licence and is an aviation historian, currently working on a history of the RAF in Germany.

My task is to set the historical background against which the presentations which follow can be viewed. The finer points of detail will be explored in those presentations and I will therefore focus on the wider-ranging activities which affected the Command as a whole.

It was in the closing few weeks of the Second World War that RAF squadrons of the 2nd Tactical Air Force swept into Germany alongside Field Marshal Montgomery's 21st Army Group. Second TAF had been specially equipped, trained and employed in close support of the ground battle but, with the formal surrender of Germany at Luneburg Heath on 5 May 1945, its squadrons and other units suddenly found themselves with a new role – that of an occupying power. The pace of life quickly changed and for a short time it was possible to celebrate the end of the war with a number of formation flypasts, the so-called "Balbo and booze" era. But there was a serious job to be done. Germany was now occupied by the Allies and the well-honed fighting machine that was 2nd TAF had to come to terms with its new role. As a result, on 15 July 1945 a new organisation, British Air Forces of Occupation, (BAFO), came into being. From the outset BAFO was organised on a composite basis with its Headquarters located at Bad Eilsen, close to the Headquarters of the newly formed British Army of the Rhine at nearby Bad Oyenhausen.

Under the command of Air Chief Marshal Sir William Sholto Douglas, BAFO comprised on its formation 4 Groups, 20 Wings and 68 Squadrons spread across 20 operational airfields in Germany and the Low Countries. BAFO's principal task was to support BAOR and carry out air policing of the British Zone of Occupation, a task made more difficult by the damage inflicted during the bombing of the war years. Moreover, there was constant disruption and turbulence as squadrons and units were disbanded, merged, relocated or re-equipped at a time when the overriding desire of BAFO's people was to return home and find new employment. Uncertainty over its future role, and even its place within the RAF, plus the loss of expertise and the dilution of skills, were serious challenges to be faced by BAFO's commanders.

Each of BAFO's Groups had an Air Disarmament Wing which carried out the search, identification and reporting of war material. The disposal of the most important material was directed by a team from Air Technical Intelligence and by June 1946 over 8,500 items of equipment had been returned to the UK. A further responsibility of BAFO was disarmament of the German aircraft industry, disposal of the signals and radar establishments and the destruction of aircraft and airfields. Almost 5,000 potentially flyable aircraft were found in the British Zone, a number of which were taken to the UK for testing. However, the most dangerous task facing the disarmament units was explosives disposal because of the poor and unstable condition of the munitions which were found. At its peak the disarmament task absorbed over 8,000 personnel and the bulk of it was completed by mid-1946.

By the end of 1947 the state of Britain's flagging economy made further cuts in the size of BAFO inevitable. Gone were the former Group and Wing HQ. The number of squadrons was reduced to 10 based at just three airfields and all under the direct operational control of the Air Headquarters at Bad Eilsen. This force should have been suitable for peacetime garrison duties but the division of Europe, institutionalised at Yalta and Potsdam, required the squadrons to move forward to patrol the Air Defence Zone established 30 miles back from the border with the German Democratic Republic. Wunstorf housed a single squadron of 16 fighter-reconnaissance Spitfires and two squadrons of Tempest Vs with a strength of 25 aircraft. A little further from the border, Gütersloh housed three squadrons with a total of 50 Tempest IIs whilst Wahn, on the banks of the Rhine, housed four Mosquito squadrons with 30 aircraft. BAFO's squadrons therefore boasted a strength of just 121 aircraft but faced an acute shortage of manpower, spare parts and equipment such that only half the aircraft could be made serviceable. Debilitated by demobilisation, the principal fear in BAFO at the end of 1947 was that the hard-won lessons of mobility and ground attack, learned in the fight across France and the Low Countries, would be too widely dispersed and forgotten.

It was over Berlin, buried deep inside the Russian Zone of Occupation, that international relations were to become increasingly strained. On 24 June 1948 the Soviet authorities closed all road and rail links to Berlin and the Western Allies set about the re-supply of the City by air. The integrity of the air corridors to Berlin was enshrined in the Quadripartite Agreement of November 1945 and Operation PLAINFARE swung into action. Over the next 12 months aircraft of the RAF, including Dakotas, Yorks, Sunderlands and later the Hastings, together with a variety of aircraft chartered from civil companies and aircraft of the USAF, kept the city supplied with food and fuel. The task necessitated substantial airfield works and BAFO was required to move out of Wunstorf and Celle to allow their use by C-54 aircraft of the USAF. The blockade was lifted on 12 May 1949 but the RAF element of the airlift continued until October to allow a stock of supplies to be accumulated in Berlin in the event of re-imposition of the blockade.

To back-track slightly, as the blockade of Berlin began so BAFO received its first jet aircraft, the diminutive Vampire. Five of BAFO's squadrons had re-equipped with the Vampire by the outbreak of the Korean War when the expansion programme began in earnest. The Vampire and the Meteor were at the forefront of the BAFO expansion, followed by the Venom which arrived from mid-1952. However, it was clear that BAFO was no longer an air force of occupation and from 1st September 1951 it reverted to the name Second Tactical Air Force or 2TAF. This title should not be confused with the Second Allied Tactical Air Force, 2 ATAF, of which you will hear more in the next presentation.

The remilitarisation of Europe in the wake of the Korean War saw 2TAF participate in many large-scale deployments and exercises. A massive programme of airfield construction began which saw the rehabilitation of a number of wartime airfields such as Jever and Oldenberg whilst many new bases were built to the west of the Rhine, the so-called "Clutch" airfields of Geilenkirchen, Wildenrath, Brüggen and Laarbruch, names which were to become synonymous with the RAF in Germany. The first of the new airfields to open was Wildenrath, which did so in January 1952. This was followed by the opening of Geilenkirchen in March 1953, Brüggen in July 1953 and finally Laarbruch by the end of 1954. In parallel with the construction of airfields, the Central European Pipeline System and its associated bulk fuel stores was built and all airfields were provided with a rail link as an alternative means of fuel and stores supply. Construction of a new "Peace Headquarters" at Rheindahlen began in April 1953 and the building was occupied in October 1954 allowing collocation of HQ 2TAF and HQ BAOR in a new Joint Headquarters.

In parallel with the airfield construction programme 2TAF's re-equipment programme continued, with delivery of the first Canadair Sabres from March 1953. However, throughout the early 1950s the aircraft accident rate was an ongoing cause for concern. Unlike the case of a Sabre, which came to grief at Oldenburg in 1956, many aircraft were totally destroyed and their crew killed in needless accidents and much effort was put into accident prevention. The arrival of the Sabre gave 2TAF a much needed swept-wing fighter capability some two years before the home-grown Hunter became available in large numbers. The swept-wing Swift was also used in Germany but in the dedicated fighter-reconnaissance role. From 1954 the Canberra was to see service in Germany, being destined to serve alongside the Hunter until the early 1970s.

However, the storm clouds were brewing for 2TAF. As the British Government wrestled with the economic backlash of the Suez Crisis the Defence White Paper of April 1957 was to have a profound effect on the size and shape of the RAF's forces in Germany. The size of 2TAF was to be reduced by half and greater reliance was to be placed on nuclear weapons. It was intended to achieve the reduction in aircraft numbers within a year and in future 2TAF would become a nuclear strike and reconnaissance force only, having lost its fighter and ground attack capability. The impact was immediate and two Hunter squadrons at Brüggen disbanded before the end of the month. Personnel on leave in the UK were told not to return to their Units and the process of hand over of airfields to the fledgling Luftwaffe was accelerated. By the end of 1958, Wahn, Celle, Bückeburg, Oldenburg, Wunstorf and Ahlhorn had all been handed back to the Luftwaffe. Overall, the squadron strength of RAF Germany fell from 36 in 1956 to just 12 in 1961. It is perhaps no coincidence that on 1 January 1959 2TAF was renamed RAF Germany.

Fortunately, the re-equipment programmes endorsed by the White Paper went ahead, the Hunter F6 arriving to equip five squadrons. Four squadrons were armed with interdictor versions of the Canberra and were able to operate in the tactical nuclear role, whilst a further three squadrons of Canberras provided a long-range reconnaissance capability. The Javelin also arrived to provide a night and all-weather air defence force. This capability was regularly tested as tension increased over Berlin and RAF Germany, together with units of the French and U.S. Air Forces, participated in Berlin contingency operations. At the height of the Berlin crisis in 1961 RAF Germany was reinforced by the permanent deployment of a Javelin squadron from Fighter Command.

From 1965 the Javelins were replaced by the Lightnings, at first based at both Geilenkirchen and Gütersloh. However, following further pressure to make economies Geilenkirchen was closed in 1968, its Lightning squadron being moved forward to Gütersloh. In the wake of the Czechoslovakian crisis of that year many improvements were made to RAF Germany's capability. The Canberras and Hunters gave way to the Harrier and the Phantom in 1970, followed by the Buccaneer in 1971. Arrival of the Jaguar in 1975 allowed the Phantoms to be re-roled to Air Defence and supersede the Lightning from early 1977. This total re-equipment saw RAF Germany's capability increase from the three combat types it fielded during the 1960s to four combat types, a situation which was to be sustained for the next 20 years.

Not only was the number of combat types increased but great efforts were made to improve the effectiveness of the available forces. Airfields were enhanced by the construction of hardened aircraft shelters and aircraft, vehicles and buildings were toned-down. Regular exercises tested war procedures and the word TACEVAL became synonymous with RAF Germany. Many techniques, such as operational turnrounds and battle-damage repair, were developed to improved aircraft availability whilst new tactics and technology were deployed to improve the effectiveness of the aircraft and their crews when in the air. Over the years the capability of aircraft, like the Jaguar, was enhanced considerably by work carried out in RAF Germany and the effectiveness of this work was proven again and again on exercises such as Red Flag, the NATO Tactical Air Meets and competitions such as the Duncan and the Salmond Trophies.

After 12 years in service with RAF Germany, the Buccaneer gave way to the Tornado from 1983, the type also supplanting a number of Jaguar squadrons in the strike/attack role. Thus, by the end of the 1980s RAF Germany comprised eight squadrons of Tornados, split between Brüggen and Laarbruch, and two squadrons of Phantoms at Wildenrath. A further two squadrons of Harrier GR3s at Gütersloh were in the process of re-equipping with the new Harrier GR5 and later the GR7. Additionally, Gütersloh housed a squadron each of Puma and Chinook support helicopters, whilst further assistance came from Rapier SAM and field squadrons of the RAF Regiment, plus a communications squadron based at Wildenrath.

Yet another turning point was reached in 1989 with the fall of the Berlin Wall and in July 1990 the British Government issued its "Options for Change" study which proposed another 50% cut in British Forces stationed in Germany. The cuts were to be implemented over a 5-year period and in November 1990 Ministers announced that it was to be Wildenrath and Gütersloh that were to close as RAF units. It was perhaps unfortunate that these announcements came at a time when a large proportion of RAF Germany, both aircraft and personnel, were deployed to the Middle East on Operation GRANBY.

Halving of the Germany-based Tornado force began in the last few months of 1991 with the disbandment or return to the UK of the squadrons based at Laarbruch. Quickly, flying operations at Wildenrath were brought to a close, the Phantoms being withdrawn from Service in early 1992. Wildenrath closed as an RAF station on 31 March 1992 and was handed over to the local German authority and I understand that it now houses a locomotive test track. Transfer of the Harrier squadrons from Gütersloh to Laarbruch took place in November 1992 and Gütersloh's final flying unit, 18 Squadron with Pumas and Chinooks, left in March 1993 before the station was handed over to the British Army in June to become the Princess Royal Barracks. Disbandment of the RAF's last overseas Command came on 31 March 1993 with a parade held in front of the JHQ building at Rheindahlen reviewed by His Royal Highness the Duke of

Edinburgh. Thereafter, HQ No. 2 Group was re-formed at Rheindahlen to command the RAF's remaining units in Germany.

Whilst the theme of our seminar today takes us up to the disbandment of RAF Germany in 1993, I must record that as a result of the 1994 Defence Costs Study, an initiative dubbed "Front Line First", it was announced that RAF Laarbruch was to close in 1999. HQ 2 Group was disbanded on 31 March 1996 and control of the Germany-based units was passed to HQ 1 Group at High Wycombe. Just a month later, publication of the 1996 Defence White Paper saw the announcement of the final withdrawal of the RAF from Germany with the news that Brüggen was to close by the year 2002. Despite the delivery of the first Tornado GR4 to Brüggen earlier this year, the 1998 Strategic Defence Review went on to announce that 17 Squadron would disband at Brüggen on 31 March next year, so accelerating the RAF's withdrawal from Germany. Thus, by 2002, after a little less than 60 years, the RAF will no longer be permanently based on German soil.

That concludes what has been a very rapid look at more than 50 years of RAF history. Perhaps it is best summed up by this short quotation from 1977:

"In fulfilling our assigned role in NATO we face impressive odds, further compounded by the troubled world in which we live. If you have ever in the past doubted the worth of your contribution you will have little cause to doubt it here. You are at the 'sharp-end' and it does not come much sharper."

RAF Brüggen Station Information Booklet 1977

2. A Continental Commitment

Group Captain Stuart Peach

Gp Capt Peach joined the RAF in 1977 after graduating from Sheffield University and 20 years later a Master's Degree at Downing College, Cambridge. The intervening years include 3,500 fast jet flying hours - many on the Tornado, PSO to the C-in-C RAF Germany, OC of IX Sqn at Brüggen and several deployments to other countries.

He is currently Director of Defence Studies (RAF) and also Executive Editor of the RAF Air Power Review.

Introduction

This chapter examines the complex legacy of the end of the Second World War in Europe for the Royal Air Force in general and the tactical squadrons in particular. This legacy shaped what was to become an important commitment for the RAF for 55 years. That forces – particularly air forces – should remain in Germany, first as forces of occupation then as NATO assigned forces for over half a century, was not an automatic assumption in 1945. Britain had always been wary of a continental commitment in peacetime, in the summer of 1945, the RAF was a global force and strategically totally over-stretched. As we shall see, the air marshals wanted the squadrons and personnel of the Second Tactical Air Force (2TAF) to return to the UK. In the event, the peacetime commitment to Germany throughout the Cold War became the dominant force in the tactical development of the RAF and shapes its professional focus to this day.

The 1945-50 period leading to the creation of NATO is explained in some detail, because this explains the 'why' of this continental commitment. Next, I trace the development to maturity of the Second Allied Tactical Air Force (TWOATAF) and highlight the subsequent reduction in British forces in Germany at the end of the Cold War. I conclude with an assessment of the legacy of the RAF's commitment to Germany as the remaining elements prepare to return to the UK.

1945

In the summer of 1945, much of western Europe lay in ruins. Hitler's Germany had been defeated and the scourge of Nazism removed, but at a very high price in blood and treasure. The RAF had made a decisive contribution across the globe. Since D-Day, the squadrons of 2TAF had operated, in John Terraine's phrase, 'at the right of the line' during the last hectic few months of the campaign in North West Europe.[1] Some squadrons had moved bases as often as 23 times from June 1944 to March 1945.[2] The wartime commanders now became post-war commanders and, as they surveyed the effects of five years of bombing upon Germany, the immediate task of reconstruction let alone reconciliation seemed to them overpowering in complexity and scale.

German infrastructure was shattered. Basic services were non-existent; food was scarce and millions of people – displaced persons – were on the move as the European continent adjusted to the post war era. Understandably, the men and women of the 80 squadrons of 2TAF RAF wanted to go home. But there was much to be done. Even by May 1945, there were ominous signs that the victorious Red Army was not preparing to go home – they were preparing for a long stay.

In this confused environment, the RAF found itself in a dilemma. In the maelstrom of Whitehall the whole question of the speed of demobilisation had become a party political issue.[3] The RAF had global responsibilities and, anyway, the war against Japan was about to reach its culminating point. Clearly the security task facing 2TAF in Germany was important, but it was very different to total war. Air policing was the order of the day. Indeed, there were those in the Air Ministry that proposed to "police" Germany from the air from the UK so that a tired and bankrupt Britain could have her airmen back.[4] But, as the realities of the devastation in Germany sank in, common sense prevailed and 2TAF concentrated on running down as quickly as possible. Nonetheless, it was important that peacetime command and control arrangements were clarified. As the Potsdam agreement was implemented after July 1945, it was apparent that an early return to the UK was out of the question for many elements of 2TAF – despite the wish to go home.

The 'Big Four' agreement at Potsdam was only reached after considerable diplomatic/political difficulty. Since 1943 there had been a number of schemes concerning 'what to do with Germany' after she had been defeated in the unconditional surrender demanded by the Casablanca declaration. Morgenthau, the US Secretary of the Treasury, proposed a 'Breguelian' solution to turn Germany into a de-militarised and de-industrialised pre-industrial pastoral land. Some historians now claim this made Germany fight on.[5] In the event at Potsdam, full responsibility for the whole of defeated Germany was granted to the US, Britain, France and Russia.[6] The agreement did not offer any clear role for the air arms of 2TAF; their common purpose had evaporated with victory on VE Day – occupation would become a British problem.

The dominion air forces wanted to go home as did the French, Belgians, Dutch, Norwegians, Czechs, Poles and others.[7] This complex and delicate task – whilst maintaining security responsibilities – was given to the newly appointed Commander 2TAF, Air Chief Marshal Sir Sholto Douglas. Until the end of the war in Europe, Douglas had been Air Officer Commander-in-Chief Coastal Command. Douglas had been appointed by Portal in July 1945 to succeed Air Marshal 'Maori' Coningham as Commander 2TAF, becoming C-in-C British Air Forces of Occupation later that month. The Headquarters was based alongside the British Army in a hotel in Bad Eilsen near Minden.

Clearly this appointment appeared to be a logical move in the post-war readjustment of the RAF. In reality it was more complex. At the end of the war, Field Marshal Montgomery became Commander-in-Chief of all British forces in Germany and he had had enough of Coningham. Tedder remained in place as Deputy Supreme Commander – in theory Montgomery's superior, but in the summer of 1945 relations between Tedder and Montgomery were very poor, so Montgomery was unlikely to accept Tedder as an interlocutor on Portal's behalf. Relations between Montgomery and Coningham had steadily worsened since 1942 when Coningham felt that Montgomery had taken all the credit in the Western Desert campaign for himself and the Eighth Army and had not properly acknowledged the role played by the Desert Air Force. When Coningham had been appointed as Commander 2TAF in the preparation for D-Day, he declined to collocate HQ 2TAF with Montgomery's Tactical HQ (as he had in the desert) and contact between the two commanders became irregular and difficult after D-Day as Montgomery's Tactical HQ (Forward) leapfrogged across France, Belgium, Holland and

Germany, dislocated from their equivalent air headquarters. During the last few hectic months of the war Coningham appeared to 'have gone off the boil' and Montgomery had – as usual – gone around the command chain and relied largely upon junior commanders such as Broadhurst, Huddleston or Embrey rather than Coningham for air advice.[8] Moreover, by this stage Coningham realised that the machinations in Whitehall meant that he was to be replaced. His final disappointment upon leaving Germany was that he felt 2TAF personnel had been slighted in the Victory Honours list.[9]

In his memoirs, *Years of Command,* Douglas recalls that Portal considered offering the C-in-C British Air Forces Occupation (BAFO) job to Bert Harris but, probably wisely, Portal concluded that Harris could and would not work with Montgomery.[10] Douglas, although reluctant to take the job, accepted because he could work with Montgomery and there was a great deal of mutual respect between them. This antagonistic relationship between air and land commanders is covered in some detail because it became a recurrent theme over the next few difficult years.

The Strategic Context
Britain had traditionally been wary of a continental commitment. Portal who stayed on as CAS until early 1946 and Tedder, the CAS designate, were keen to focus on the traditional British strategic priorities of the protection of Empire, sea control of the Mediterranean and the traditional trade routes to India. In air matters they were determined to develop an air strategy based upon strategic bombing and atomic bombs – see below.[11] The Germany problem was not top of the agenda. Indeed, as Paul Cornish makes clear in his excellent survey of British Defence Policy between 1945 and 1951, Germany was number four on the British Defence Policy shopping list. Furthermore, shortly after the use of the atomic bomb by the USAAF against Japan, Portal (soon to become Britain's atomic supremo) and Tedder argued long and hard in Chiefs of Staff Committee for Britain to rely on an independent strategic bombing air strategy.[12]

This focus upon strategic air power was to bedevil the units that remained in Germany. Tactical air power was to be neglected in terms of design, procurement, manning and equipment for years to come. As this chapter will make clear, the RAF muddled through with tactical aircraft throughout the Cold War. Despite a justly deserved reputation for tactical excellence and professional competence, rarely did the RAF have the right equipment for the job. Priorities lay elsewhere – in the build-up and maintenance of the V-Force as the UK's strategic deterrent. This factor makes the achievements of the RAF in Germany all' the more impressive. Returning to 1945, however, the rundown of 2TAF and BAFO as the Command HQ at Bad Eilsen was retitled in July 1945 proceeded apace: by the end of 1945, the RAF in Germany was down to 10 Squadrons from a strength of 80 in May 1945.

The task for air power, however, was by no means over. In addition to routine air patrols and training, Douglas faced a number of serious issues; issues which posed a different but, nonetheless important, series of leadership and command challenges. Apart from dealing with Montgomery who 'ruled' autocratically from his Schloss near Osnabruck with little or no consultation with his senior colleagues, was the vexed question of the disbandment of the Luftwaffe. This task was given to Air Marshal Sir Philip Wigglesworth and was completed with efficiency and sensitivity; he was rewarded with appointment as Commander-in-Chief BAFO in May 1946. Douglas was criticised by Whitehall, however, for dragging his feet – there was little mood for sensitivity back in London. Meanwhile, down at unit level, airmen chafed at the inactivity, reacting to increasingly frustrated letters from home and the drab reality of life in occupied Germany in 1945.[13] There were a number of flying accidents and, as the truth about the nature of the Nazi regime emerged, relations with the local population were difficult at best. Although Douglas did not rigidly enforce Field Marshal Montgomery's famous "no fraternisation" rule[14], as 1945 wore on Anglo/German relations in the British zone became difficult.[15]

Against this complex background of strategic tension and economic adjustment to harsh peacetime realities, the change of title from 2TAF to British Air Force of Occupation (BAFO) became more than symbolic. The winter of 1945/46 was long and hard; conditions for displaced persons worsened steadily. German people and refugees were starving to death in their thousands. The elderly, the sick and the lame were being herded across into the British zone from the Soviet zone to reduce the burden on the Soviet system in the east – and for propaganda reasons. In consequence, one of the many roles undertaken by BAFO was delivery of food aid in what we would now call humanitarian operations. Even this caused difficulties amongst the airmen as it appeared that the Germans were being better fed than the British people, since conditions in the UK worsened during early 1946 and rationing became more extensive. Nor is there any doubt that the UK's precarious international financial situation influenced both foreign and defence policy. Bevin, the Foreign Secretary and other senior members of Attlee's Cabinet were deeply concerned over Soviet intentions. But, in a presumably coincidental re-run of the infamous 10 year rule, the Joint Intelligence Committee optimistically predicted that the Soviet Union would not be in a position to launch an invasion of Western Europe until 1955-56. Although based on sound technical intelligence advice, Britain was virtually bankrupt and this assessment fitted the need for financial restraint at a time of strategic overstretch.[16]

Down at the tactical level, frustration also showed in the day to day "nitpicking" administration that befell the post-war air force in Germany. This was known by airmen serving at the time as the "Uxbridge" factor, it was not a compliment.[17] Douglas worked hard for his men and put a great deal of personal effort into ensuring both the swift return of allied personnel and in his attempts to obtain security guarantees from reluctant Soviet officials for the safety of his gallant Polish and Czech airmen before they disappeared into an unknown future in the Soviet zone. In fact, the orderly withdrawal and transformation of BAFO from a 2TAF internationally manned wartime force into a single service occupation force is excellent testimony to Douglas's measured leadership skills.

The Cold War
Throughout 1945 and early 1946, relations with the Soviet forces steadily worsened. In addition to the alarming condition of people inside Germany at the strategic level, the main sticking point was Berlin. The Allies were determined to maintain security and exercise their rights over the divided city in accordance with the Potsdam agreement. The Soviets were equally determined to exercise control their way. Douglas did not like this political element to his post. He railed at spending so much time in negotiation with the Russians over what he believed were essentially political questions.[18] He wrote to his wife that he wished to retire. Instead, he was persuaded by Prime

Minister Attlee to accept the post of British Commissioner in Germany when Montgomery returned to London to take up his appointment as Chief of the Imperial General Staff. Douglas did not want the job and twice tried to refuse it, but accepted it following the intervention of the Prime Minister out of a sense of duty and assumed his new title in April 1946. Despite their position as senior colleagues, Montgomery did not give Douglas a handover. Montgomery did not even show Douglas his 'special memorandum' on the German situation which had been circulated to the Cabinet; he just returned to England, the day Douglas arrived back to take up his new post.[19] As Commissioner, the political difficulties surrounding his post intensified with the Nuremberg Trials as did the practical problems surrounding C-in-C BAFO, Sir Philip Wigglesworth. With just 10 Squadrons, poor serviceability and poor morale, BAFO was hopelessly outnumbered by the Soviet Air Forces who had rapidly occupied former Luftwaffe airfields and were mounting constant and aggressive patrols. Views from Germany at the time, the silken phrases of JIC reassurance did not appear to recognise reality.

Throughout 1947 and early 1948 there were a number of potentially dangerous incidents involving BAFO and Soviet aircraft. BAFO commanders knew they were outnumbered and also knew that the Soviets had sufficient in-place ready forces to launch a pre-emptive attack without warning. Berlin remained the flashpoint. In May 1948, the Soviets closed the land and rail corridors; Berlin was isolated. In the days that followed, confusion reigned. Some historians argue that Rex Waite, Air Commodore Plans, wrote the plan that first suggested that Berlin could be resupplied by air. In fact the US were already working on contingency plans for an airlift led by General Lucius Clay the energetic and charismatic US Commissioner. He decided to go for the airlift option and thus the Berlin airlift began. The rest is a matter for record. As the 50th Anniversary events of 1998 have demonstrated, it was a difficult and dangerous mission: 18 RAF and 21 civilian airmen died. The RAF's contribution was outstanding flying over $^1/_2$ million tons of supplies over a year of confrontation. Aircraft alone had kept Berlin supplied during the long hard winter of 1948/49 and the Allies had won the first Cold War confrontation. At the grand strategic level, the Berlin airlift demonstrated to the world the intransigence of the Soviet authorities.

The Birth of NATO

At a stroke, the Berlin airlift muted the US isolationists who wanted to withdraw from Europe, it bolstered US commitment to the Marshall Plan and led to calls for rearmament across the political spectrum. The Dunkirk Treaty of 1947 had offered security guarantees between Britain and France, which had been expanded by the Brussels Pact of 1948 to include Belgium and Holland. These European moves paved the way for the creation of NATO. As the Cold War solidified, the Washington Treaty of April 1949 set the conditions for the creation of NATO as a military organisation. Although some remained reluctant to sanction rearmament, the Soviet-backed invasion of South Korea in 1950 graphically demonstrated that the Cold War could rapidly turn into a hot one and silenced the doubters. The success of the North Korean forces demonstrated to BAFO the need for defence in depth, not simply forward defence. As a result, the programme for airfield construction around the Rhine area was accelerated with the bases to the west of Cologne known collectively as the "Clutch" airfields completed by 1955.[20]

Driven by the apparent military stalemate in Korea and Soviet intransigence on all fronts, NATO defence ministers and military chiefs met in Lisbon in 1952 to put military meaning into NATO. As a result, the Lisbon force goals were announced which aspired to the creation of tactical air forces throughout the Central Region of NATO to deter and, if necessary, counter Soviet aggression. The force goals were translated into a medium term plan which envisaged 600+ RAF tactical aircraft deployed in Germany. Although taken seriously by planners, this commitment was wholly unrealistic given the constrained levels of defence spending and Britain's other global commitments. Britain was strategically stretched on all fronts. The pot of independence was bubbling over across the British Empire into direct action and confrontation. New aircraft, equipment and weapons were beginning to appear, but not as quickly as the companies promised and were often not as capable as promised. Indeed, the deliberate policy of sharing contracts to a wide number of suppliers led inevitably to small production runs, several mediocre aircraft and little thought to weapon system integration. Although world class aircraft such as the Canberra and Hunter were beginning to appear by the mid-1950s, the Meteor and Vampire were no match for emerging US and Soviet aircraft such as the F-84, F-86, MiG-15 and MiG-17.

The Second Allied Tactical Air Force

Despite economic and strategic constraint, the RAF build-up continued during 1952-55 reaching a post-war peak of 35 Squadrons.[21] Meanwhile the Cold War realities and the Lisbon commitment meant that burden sharing could become a reality and 2TAF Squadrons could become multinational once more. In 1953, the Joint Headquarters at Rheindahlen was completed in record time and became the home for the Second Allied Tactical Air Force (TWOATAF) working alongside the Northern Army Group (NORTHAG). At first, British officers dominated the Headquarters, but for practical as well as altruistic reasons, the RAF played a major role in the re-formation of the Belgian Air Force and Royal Netherlands Air Force with 'soft' deals on RAF aircraft and assistance with flying training. Belgian and Dutch staff officers with wartime experience quickly appeared at Rheindahlen giving an international feel to the Headquarters.

A more strategic readjustment took place in 1955 with the rearming of Germany, the re-formation of the Luftwaffe, and the absorption of Luftwaffe staff officers into Headquarters TWOATAF from 1955. The role of Headquarters TWOATAF was the execution of NATO strategy and military policy for all assigned forces. COM-TWOATAF became a Principal Subordinate Commander (PSC) within the Central Region of NATO. In peacetime, COMTWOATAF exercised operational control (OPCON) of air defence units – comprising fighters, surface-to-air missile belts and extensive air defence radar networks. This critical responsibility remained in place until 1991 (see Air Chief Marshal Palin's paper elsewhere in this volume for details). Should war break out, COMTWOATAF would exercise operational control of all assigned forces within his area of responsibility. The scale of this task should not be underestimated. By the 1970s, with large numbers of reinforcements from continental USA, this command numbered over 2,500 aircraft. Thus, the development of a coherent tactical doctrine and the establishment of a sensible exercise and training programme for TWOATAF units made COMTWOATAF one of the major senior command tasks held by the RAF – and one that is often neglected in 'coffee table' books on the post-war RAF.

Returning to the historical flow of events, as the vast costs of the V-Bomber programme in treasure, training and personnel hit home, the Medium Term Programme and Lisbon Force goals collapsed. Space precludes a description of the post-Suez strategic and technical background, but the Sandys Defence Review of 1957 exposed the impossibility of meeting all the tasks facing the Service. Not for the first or last time, 2TAF units in Germany were seen as an easy target for cuts – the V-Force and strategic deterrent had to be protected. In the organisational chaos that followed, the RAF handed back a number of well found bases to the Luftwaffe.[22] More cuts to RAF strength in Germany followed in the late 1950s, until a Cold War steady state of 12 Squadrons was reached by 1962. The outclassed and outdated Meteors, Vampires and Venoms had gone as had the Sabres supplied by Canada under the Military Assistance Programme. By the early 1960s, the Command was re-equipped with a mix of Hunter and Swift for light attack and tactical reconnaissance, Canberra B16 and B18 versions for nuclear strike and medium bombing, Canberra PR7 for photographic reconnaissance and Javelin aircraft supplemented later by Lightning F2As for air defence.[23] The nuclear role for RAF squadrons in Germany was one of the critical factors in maintaining British influence (see Air Cdre Wilkinson's paper on Canberra strike operations elsewhere in this volume). Allied air forces employed a similar mix of fast jet aircraft. Thus, by the 1960s TWOATAF was established as a key component of NATO's Cold War tactical air forces.

Throughout the 1960s and 1970s the reputation of TWOATAF for professional competence and tactical expertise was second to none. The Command stood ready as the Cold War crises over Berlin, Cuba and Czechoslovakia threatened to erupt into war. A true front line spirit of working and playing hard developed. Indeed, many of the important and enduring successes of NATO's air forces during the Cold War originated in TWOATAF. The Tactical Evaluation programme, colloquially known as TACEVAL, ensured the highest standards of training and readiness. Similarly, the NATO Central Region Tactical Leadership Programme (TLP) established in the 1970s played a major role in educating aircrew in the composite tactics that did so much to shape the air campaign during the Gulf War.[24]

Command and control arrangements evolved over the years to reflect the growing internationalisation of the Headquarters. As the RAF's strength in Germany reduced, the command arrangement of two Group Headquarters, Number 2 Group and 83 Group, which had coped with the rapid expansion and equally rapid retrenchment of the 1950s proved untenable and the RAF's Command headquarters was moved to Rheindahlen and retitled as Headquarters RAF Germany with the appropriate 'Keepers of the Peace' motto in 1959.[25] The Commander-in-Chief was double-hatted as COMTWOATAF. This arrangement, with a 2 Star RAF Deputy Commander as the de facto Air Officer Commanding, worked well and lasted from 1959 to 1993. Inevitably as the Cold War continued and the partner air forces grew in strength, British command of 2ATAF was challenged, particularly since some RAF C-in-Cs appeared to focus exclusively on National responsibilities in RAFG and neglect their NATO duties in TWOATAF. In 1963, the sole RAF responsibility for command was formally challenged by NATO and, in consequence, from 1963 to 1966 COMTWOATAF was a Belgian general. This interlude was not regarded as a success by those serving in TWOATAF at the time and the nations elected to return to the status quo ante and a British Commander in 1966; a position which remained extant until the disbandment of TWOATAF in 1993.[26]

In addition to his extensive day-to-day operational responsibilities, COMTWOATAF also acted in a strictly national capacity as the Chairman of the Commander-in-Chiefs Committee (Germany) (CICC(G)), a rotating appointment with C-in-C BAOR. This unique group consisted of the RAF and BAOR Commanders-in-Chief, the UK ambassadors from the Central Region nations and the UK Military Representative and Permanent Representative at ambassador level from Brussels. This group proved extremely successful throughout the Cold War offering an outstanding political/diplomatic/military axis, enabling the UK to "sing from a single sheet" during the many and varied crises of the Cold War. All senior commanders who served on CICC(G) speak warmly of its relevance and importance in maintaining a coherent UK position.

The strategic earthquake of the French withdrawal from the integrated military structure in 1966 rippled outwards to Rheindahlen. Although relations between the RAF and FAF remained cordial, French presence was reduced to a minimum in the form of liaison officers. The US, too, felt somewhat marginalised by UK domination within HQ2ATAF and, as a result of the significant US Air Forces based within the 2ATAF area of responsibility, the post of Deputy C-in-C of Staff Operations was allocated to the USAF in

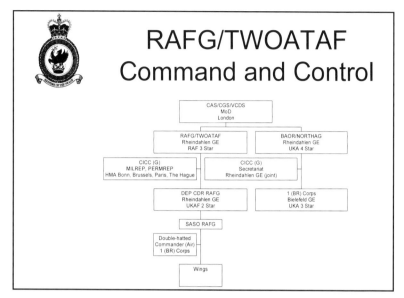

Figure 1

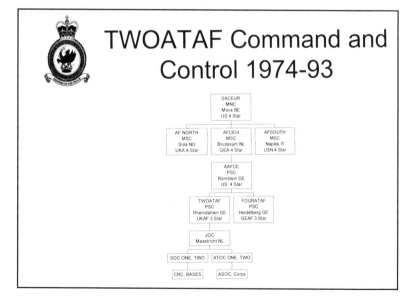

Figure 2

1977. Thus, by 1977, 2ATAF was a truly integrated international headquarters of five nations with subordinate headquarters and units located across the Central Region of NATO, as shown in Figure 2.

The Soviet invasion of Afghanistan in 1979 and serious tension in Poland in 1980 and 1981 confirmed that at any moment the Cold War could turn into a hot one. When the ingredients of conflict in the Middle East and the shooting down of the Korean Airlines Boeing 747 by the Soviet Air Force in 1983 are added, the early 1980s was one of the most dangerous times of the Cold War. In addition to enhanced realistic training such as Exercise Red Flag in the Nevada Ranges and low-level training in Goose Bay Canada, NATO maintained constant vigilance through a regular series of Command Post Exercises (CPX). The annual exercise which tested TWOATAF command and control (C2) of its nuclear and conventional forces and subordinate headquarters was codenamed ABLE ARCHER. A misunderstanding by the KGB, during Exercise ABLE ARCHER 1983, nearly led to a strategic miscalculation by the Soviet Union. As the Exercise progressed, CPX procedures were matched by enhanced security and unit moves following the terrorist massacre of US Marines in Lebanon and continuing IRA operations against British Forces Germany. This combination of exercise signals traffic and real unit moves was misinterpreted by the KGB and the Soviet Union placed their forces in Germany on full alert, fearing an imminent attack by NATO. It was a closer run thing than those serving in TWOATAF realised at the time.[27]

Fortunately, the long years of training exercises helped to retain the edge of deterrence within NATO as the Soviet Union struggled to retain control over the Warsaw Pact. By 1986-7 as the arms control process gathered political momentum and the 'Velvet Revolution' took hold across Eastern Europe, the writing was on the wall for the Warsaw Pact – if not visible to the military units deployed forward in East Germany who continued to bring in new and more capable equipment. By 1989, when the Berlin Wall was removed without violence or war, the TWOATAF motto: *'Parcere subjectis et debellare superbos'* (spare the oppressed and subjugate the tyrant) seemed an appropriate epithet for over 35 years of international co-operation between air forces.

The Legacy of TWOATAF
COMTWOATAF was one of the most influential NATO command

posts held by the RAF since the Second World War. In addition to the daily exercise of air policing and control duties, he had extremely important nuclear and conventional attack command responsibilities. Diplomatic and civil/military functions were exercised by CICC(G) as mentioned earlier but, above all, COMTWOATAF offered a UK view and a seat at the table to balance the influence of the USAF located at Ramstein. Moreover, within senior UK military circles, COMTWOATAF could offer a broader view – taking the European perspective into account. This view was either welcomed or ignored in Whitehall depending on the priorities of the moment.

In military terms squabbles over doctrine between TWO and FOURATAF in the early 1970s persuaded a doubtful Supreme Allied Commander Europe to create a 'new' air headquarters at Ramstein in Southern Germany to co-ordinate and allocate all tactical 'air' in the Central Region.[28] Headquarters Allied Air Forces Central Europe (HQ AAFCE) was established in 1974 under USAF 4 star command. This commander was also doubled-hatted as Commander-in-Chief USAF in Europe (CINCUSAFE). Largely as a result of the size of the RAF contribution to TWOATAF, the RAF gained a 2 star post in the new headquarters as Deputy Chief of Staff Operations with other staff posts at Ramstein. Institutional tension between NATO headquarters

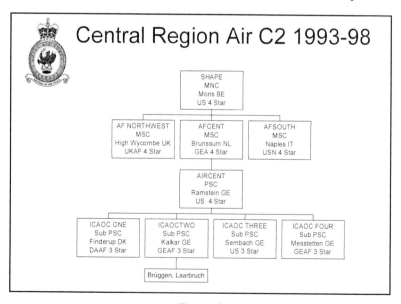

Figure 3

over tactics and doctrine surfaced regularly. Following the experience of Vietnam, the USAF pushed for a global doctrine of medium level tactics. The UK, influencing the TWOATAF position, insisted on maintaining low-level high speed flying to penetrate the dense surface-to-air defences of the Warsaw Pact.

Both tactics were tested in another region immediately at the end of the Cold War. Both worked during the Gulf War against Iraq. The low-level night attack techniques pioneered by the RAF in TWOATAF employing platform/weapon combinations such as Tornado with the JP 233 airfield denial weapon set the conditions to allow the US to prosecute its attack operations flown at medium level. These attacks were enabled by conditions of air supremacy – partly established by the early low-level attacks. Thus, it would be wrong to ascribe success to either tactic – it was the mix of tactics which worked. Furthermore, the legacy of international co-operation which was the hallmark of TWOATAF has helped to shape the C2 arrangements and coalition doctrine and procedures for both the Gulf War (and subsequent coalition operations in Iraq) and air operations in the Balkans.

Conclusion

A presence in Germany by the RAF for over half a century could not have been predicted by even the most visionary of airmen in 1945. As we approach the millennium, the British Government has decided to withdraw all RAF units from Germany by 2002.[29] The British Army remain with an Armoured Division and extensive Corps troops supporting the NATO Allied Command Europe Rapid Reaction Corps (ARRC), command of which is held by the British Army. When the RAF withdrawal is complete, the many years of air/land integration between the RAF and what was the British Army of the Rhine will be broken. Of course, RAF squadrons will still train with the British Army and European partners, but it will not be the intimate spirit of understanding and co-operation that was established in Germany in the 1960s-1980s by RAFG units and 1(British) Corps. Furthermore, the retreat to the mainland UK for the RAF marks the end of a large scale permanent overseas presence for the Service for the first time in its history.

The RAF can be proud of its contribution to NATO's Central Region expressed through the commitment, courage and professionalism of the men and women of 2TAF, BAFO, TWOATAF and RAF

Germany. As the RAF Ensign is hauled down at RAF Brüggen in 2002, an important, indeed critical, chapter of RAF history is complete. Only time will tell if the next generation of airmen and airwomen can afford to ignore a continental commitment.

Footnotes:

1   J. Terraine *The Right of the Line,* Hodder 1985 remains arguably the best book on the RAF's overall performance in the Second World War.

2   See C. F. Shores *2 TAF,* Osprey, London, 1970 for details.

3   See M. Gilbert, *The Day the War Ended,* Hamilton, London, 1995 or B. Turner *When Daddy Came Home,* Hutchinson, 1995 for a description of the searing effect of adjusting to the post-war reality of 1945.

4   Tedder visited Berlin in May 1945 and realised this idea was nonsense – Germany was not some distant small colonial outpost. The scheme to resurrect colonial air policing was quietly dropped as impractical.

5   Goebbels used the leaded details of the Morgenthau plan to exhort Germans to greater sacrifice in the winter of 1944-45.

6   For a clear description of the acrimony surrounding the victorious allies at Potsdam, see J. Charmley, *Churchill's Grand Alliance,* Hodder & Stoughton, London, 1995, p.179-184.

7   In May 1945, in addition to the 'majority' RAF, 2TAF comprised 5 French, 3 Czech, 6 Polish, 2 Dutch, 2 Belgian, 2 Norwegian, 2 Australian, 3 New Zealand, and 19 Canadian Squadrons – a truly international force. See C. F. Shores, op cit.

8   Interview with Vincent Orange, Coningham's biographer, Canterbury NZ, May 1999.

9   See V. Orange, *Coningham,* USAF, Washington, 1991, p.239.

10 Viewed from the contemporary perspective it seems incredible that Portal should propose Harris for the C-in-C post in Germany, but there were few posts that Harris could fill and at this stage he had not decided to retire.

11 See E. Bramall, *The Chiefs* Brasseys, 1992, Chapter 9 (266-306) for a description of battles in Chiefs' of Staff Committee in 1945 and 1946.

12 See P. Cornish, *British Military Planning for the Defence of Germany 1945-50,* Macmillan, London, 1996 for details of strategic thinking, B. Cathcart *Test of Greatness, Britain's Struggle for the Atomic Bomb,* John Murray, London, 1994, p.15 for Portal's role and D. Lee *The RAF in Germany 1945-78* AHB(RAF), 1979 for details of command appointments.

13 There are a number of recent excellent works which give a flavour for life in 1945 in the immediate aftermath of total war. See, in particular: Gilbert, and Turner op cit.

14 See P. Mann *Comeback – Germany 1945-52,* Macmillan, London, 1980 for an excellent account of military life in occupied Germany.

15 Despite the difficulties, the British came out of the experience of occupation with respect on all sides. British administration of occupied Germany was seen to be fair and just. Testimony to British positive influence was that the 1949 Basic Law (Grundgesetz) which shapes the German Constitution to this day was crafted by British constitutional lawyers attached to the British forces of occupation.

16 Cornish, op cit, p.33.

17 RAF Uxbridge, North West of London was and is a major RAF Administrative unit. Towards the end of the war "platoons" of RAF Warrant Officers were despatched from Uxbridge to re-establish 'discipline' amongst the 2TAF units. In particular the RAF hierarchy did not approve of the 2TAF 'habit' of wearing Army battledress – a sensible precaution since many 2TAF groundcrew wearing RAF battledress were shot having been mistaken for Germans in the forward area. Other Uxbridge innovations included

the re-introduction of room inspections and drill. These Warrant Officers were not popular – especially with NCO aircrew. Source: interviews with veterans.

18 See Douglas, Ibid, p.163.

19 See, N. Hamilton, *Monty, Vol. 3,* Sceptre, London, 1986, p.624-626.

20 The airfields at Brüggen, Geilenkirchen, Laarbruch and Wildenrath were completed between 1953 and 1955 by the RAF Airfield Construction Branch and remained the centre of gravity for the RAF throughout the Cold War.

21 This was a post-war 'spike' in strength. No sooner had the squadrons formed in Germany, than the 1957 Sandys White Paper cut 2TAF in half – back down to 18 Squadrons. Personnel on leave in the UK were simply told not to return to Germany, chaos and confusion reigned – NATO was furious. Cuts continued reaching a Cold War steady state of 12 RAF Squadrons in Germany in 1962.

22 Airfields across the northern half of Germany were handed back to the Luftwaffe: Jever, Oldenburg, Ahlhorn, Fassberg, Celle, Wunstorf, Detmold and Koln/Wahn were all handed back between 1955 and 1957.

23 The Canberra, Hunter and Lightning proved very successful and as good as their US or Soviet counterparts. The Swift was not a success and the Javelin a good platform but not a good weapon system. See D. Lee, op cit for details.

24 Post-war analysis of the Gulf War clearly shows that the doctrine, tactics and procedures developed in TWOATAF shaped the air campaign.

25 The 'new' RAF headquarters at Goch near Kleve was never occupied. It now forms the Headquarters for NATO's Reaction Forces Air Staff. The Headquarters at Koln/Wahn is now Headquarters Tactical Air Command Luftwaffe (GAFTAC).

26 The exception being the final COMTWOATAF, Major General Friedrich Busch, German Air Force who held the post from April to July 1993 after Air Marshal Sir 'Sandy' Wilson returned to the UK to take up his post as the Air Member for Personnel in the rank of Air Chief Marshal.

27 See R. M. Gates, *From the Shadows,* Simon & Schuster, New York, 1995, p.270-273 for details.

28 The COMTWOATAF of the day was sceptical of the need and said so, but the US view prevailed. Interview Air Chief Marshal Sir Nigel Maynard, May 1993.

29 See Cmd 3223, the Statement of Defence Estimates 1996. This decision was confirmed by the Labour Government during the 1998 Strategic Defence Review.

3. The Principles of Air Defence
Air Chief Marshal Sir Roger Palin KCB OBE

After National Service as a Subaltern with the Parachute Regiment, Sir Roger graduated from Cambridge and joined the RAF in 1963. His operational tours include two in Germany (Lightning and Phantom) and he was C-in-C RAF Germany when the Berlin Wall came down in 1989. His final RAF appointment was as Air Member for Personnel 1991/3.

When one thinks of air defence, one instinctively thinks of military hardware – fighter aircraft, radars, guns and missiles – and of course the men and women who man and service the machinery, particularly the fighter pilots, who over the years, rightly or wrongly, have captured the imagination of the public. Where air defence of the UK is concerned, this is not an inaccurate thought process, because the history and nature of UK air defence has been dominated by on the one hand technology in the race to develop equipment to counter an ever evolving threat, and on the other by our island geography which placed a premium on fighters. Air Defence of the Homeland was also, perceptually at least, uniquely the province of the Royal Air Force. These were very much the themes which pervaded the Historical Society's earlier seminar *Defending Northern Skies.*[1]

The situation for the Royal Air Force in the air defence role in Germany was very different, where politics was a far stronger factor and where the RAF, although fulfilling some uniquely national responsibilities, was operating as one member of a fully integrated international team. This situation arose from two sources, the legacy of WW2 on the one hand, and the establishment of NATO and the development of its integrated air defence system on the other. I intend to deal with this subject, therefore, in two parts; first the political dimension, focusing particularly on air policing and air access to

Berlin, and secondly the military dimension and more specifically concepts and the role the RAF played in these. I will then draw some broad conclusions as to determinants and achievements from a historical perspective.

Defence of one's homeland, including defence against aerial attack, is often cited as the first duty of national government. In peacetime, air defence means the responsibility for and means to police one's own airspace, which by extrapolation becomes a symbol of national sovereignty. Even within NATO's integrated air defence system, it was an accepted principle that the nations carried out their own air policing, and supplied their own air defence assets, unless they chose to make other national arrangements/agreements.[2]

Only the Federal Republic of Germany (FRG) was denied this right, with the responsibility for peacetime air policing falling to the Tripartite Nations – the USA, France, and the UK. This arose, as has already been mentioned in a wider context, from the Potsdam Agreement which divided Germany at the end of WW2 into Zones of Occupation with the concomitant security responsibilities. However, it continued to apply even after the Paris Agreements of 1954 established the FRG as a sovereign state, and the General Relations Treaty with the other half of the old Germany, the German Democratic Republic, of 1972 paved the way for entry into the United Nations and other international institutions, such as the International Civil Aviation Authority, as an independent and fully sovereign nation.

Why was this? It was not as if the newly reconstituted Luftwaffe was not capable of taking on the task militarily, even if its build-up to the planned scale and capability took many years longer than originally envisaged. Nor were they without encouragement from certain quarters in the UK to take over the full responsibilities, so that the Air Ministry could reap the financial benefits of a smaller military presence in the FRG. Indeed in 1957 it had been decided at Cabinet level to withdraw all our fighter squadrons from Germany by 1961, against the advice of successive Commanders-in-Chief and Ambassadors supported by the Foreign Office, a decision which was only reversed in 1962 after many years of argument.[3] The reasons were clearly political, not military.

There were three aspects to the security responsibilities which the Tripartite Powers assumed for their Occupation Zones at the end of WW2 – air policing which fell to the RAF, control of the inter-zonal border, which was the responsibility of the Ambassador, and ensuring free access to Berlin (itself divided into four zones) which was a joint responsibility. Although in many ways these were discrete functions, with separate command arrangements and exercised separately, politically they tended to be considered as integral parts of the Quadripartite Rights and Responsibilities for Germany as a whole and for Berlin which the four Powers – the USA, France, the UK, and the Soviet Union – assumed in 1945. These Quadripartite Rights and Responsibilities were an immensely valuable political tool, providing leverage on the Germans, a channel for dealing with the Soviet Union and through them exerting some influence on the GDR, a means outside the integrated military structure of NATO for exercising militarily with the French, and an underpinning for the UK's continuing importance as a leading player in European security matters. This was demonstrated most clearly in the early 1970s at the time of Chancellor Brandt's Ostpolitik, when the Quadripartite Declaration which accompanied the General Relations Treaty between the two states of Germany already referred to, and the Quadripartite Agreement on Berlin helped to shape Ostpolitik in a way which tied the FRG firmly into the Western camp.[4] Again more recently, at the time of German reunification, the Quadripartite Powers in the Two-plus-Four talks played a central role in determining the shape of that epochal event.

Thus it was that the RAF held a small number of aircraft at a very high alert state (either 2 mins in the cockpit on the ORP, or 5 mins in the Battle Flight hangar, never less) not just in the immediate post-war years but right the way through to the moment of German reunification in the autumn of 1990. The command chain was entirely Royal Air Force, from the Commander-in-Chief through the operations staff at HQ RAFG, to RAF Wing Commander Sector Controllers at the Sector Operation Centres. German Intercept controllers were introduced in 1958, indeed over the years some CRCs came under German command, but there was always a RAF intercept controller available for the Battle Flight, and the command authority always remained with the RAF. A small force, but one whose political value was out of all proportion to its size. It was a similar situation with the responsibilities for ensuring free access to Berlin, which were exercised annually with our US and French colleagues. This comprised flights of fighters from the three Allied

Powers, with air-to-air refuelling as required, escorting air transport aircraft on simulated penetrations of the Air Corridors. The exercises took place in FRG airspace because it had become the accepted policy not to send fighter aircraft down the corridors except for real. How effective this operation would have been militarily is open to question, but it undoubtedly sent a strong political signal of Allied resolve.

Ironically, the legal basis for the Tripartite Powers continuing to police FRG airspace, particularly after the Paris Agreements conferred full sovereignty on the Federal Republic, were anything but robust, unlike the air corridors which were formally established by the four powers shortly after the war. In fact, because the rights to conduct air policing which had been assumed in 1945 were not specifically abrogated under the Paris Agreements, they were allowed to continue until a de facto position wherefore the former occupying powers continued to retain military responsibilities for what were their former zones of occupation was tolerated. A semblance of a legal basis for the right to police FRG airspace was to be found in the Settlement Convention which stated that in relation to the exercise of their responsibilities relating to Germany as a whole, the three Powers would continue to exercise control with respect to aircraft of the USSR using FRG airspace.[5] This tripartite control was extended by the then Chancellor, Dr Adenauer, in an important, but unpublished, memorandum in which he agreed that the FRG should obtain consent from the three Powers for flights by military aircraft of Satellite countries in FRG airspace and to consult them before authorising similar flights by civil aircraft.[6] Thus this extraordinary situation whereby, uniquely in NATO, three Allied Powers exercised effective control over all Soviet and Satellite aircraft in FRG airspace, despite FRG sovereignty, owed more to precedent than to legality. It has always been a source of wonder to me that the FRG did not press this matter further, particularly at the time of Ostpolitik. In fact it took unification to correct this anomalous situation.

Turning now to the more military aspects of air defence, the immediate post-war years were of course dominated by the operational requirement to provide all embracing security for all British forces, including the Army, in the British Zone of Occupation, and the inadequacy of the equipment in theatre so to do. Rudimentary Ground Control radar (Type 70), aircraft not ideally suited to air superiority duties (Tempest V and Spitfire XIV), no night fighter squadrons (although there was a requirement to maintain a trained and equipped organisation for the control and operation of night fighters), the requirement to be proficient in a number of roles and to be ready for deployment out of theatre, either to Austria or even further afield. These years were also dominated by a growing realisation of the Soviet Union's hegemonic aspirations on the one hand, and the continuous pressure for reductions in BAFO for financial reasons on the other, both of which inexorably led towards a more collective approach to security, nowhere more so than in air defence. Indeed as early as March 1948 there was a realisation among the newly formed Benelux combination that their primary need was for a common system of air defence. Interestingly, though perhaps not surprisingly, they looked to the UK for guidance, assistance and co-ordination of a common system, in which methods and equipment would be standardised on the RAF pattern.[7]

The history of the subsequent years was one of increasing internationalisation of the air defence system, eventually fully integrated under NATINADS, the slow introduction of more capable fighters (Meteor NFX1, Sabres, Hunters, Javelins, Lightnings, and finally Phantoms) although rarely the latest marques, a minimalist SAM presence (Tigercat, then Bloodhound and finally Rapier), devoted to our own short range defensive requirements, and a continual reduction in the resources committed to the role. When we finally withdrew from the air defence role under the 'Options for Change' exercise in response to German unification, we fielded a couple of 10 AE squadrons, a Rapier squadron at each main operating base, one Sector Commander and a handful of Sector Controllers, and a small staff at HQ. Yet despite this comparatively small contribution in resource terms, we maintained our leading position in terms of influence. No doubt this was helped by holding responsibility for air policing, as already discussed, and probably also from the fact that the C-in-C RAFG normally held the COMTWOATAF appointment. I have already given one example of how the other nations tended to look to the RAF for a lead; another occurred in the 1960s, when for reasons of international diplomacy it was decided that the C-in-C RAFG would not be COMTWOATAF, and a Belgian Air Force General was appointed, with the C-in-C RAFG retaining his national air policing responsibilities. The experiment lasted one appointment and it was the other nations who unanimously called for the return to the status quo ante, which I think speaks for itself.

Concerning concepts of operation, these were again very different to the UK, where because of geography and the nature of the all round threat, fighters provide the first line of defence supported by a ground environment of GCI radars and point defence of key high value targets. Although fighters predominated in the early post-war years on Continental Europe, this was due to the lack of a comprehensive ground environment and the underdeveloped state of surface to air missiles. When these latter were developed and introduced into service, the concept gradually changed to one in which the ground environment predominated, with a comprehensive and overlapping radar coverage, a series of missile belts, both high (NIKE) and low (HAWK), HIDACZES (high intensity ac control zones) to assist with Army Corps low-level air defences, with the fighters acting principally as a second line of defence. In fact, jamming would have made integrated fighter/SAM operations nigh on impossible. Again it is one of the ironies of the air defence situation on the Continent that the UK, despite its leading role, did not participate in the primary defence means, contributing nothing to the missile belts other than Bloodhound, which were employed as extended short range air defence of the Clutch stations, contributed little to the NATINAD radar chain, other than the controllers already referred to, and focused on fighters, and these in ever decreasing numbers. And yet again, despite this minimalist contribution, the RAF exerted enormous influence in determining and developing the concepts of operations. To my personal knowledge, the RAF played a leading role in redesigning the fighter high- and low-level search patterns, in developing autonomous operation procedures, in evolving the 2ATAF SOPs (Standard Operating Procedures) for mixed fighter formations, in setting up the Tactical Leadership Programme and the Combined Air Operations concepts which flowed from that. Again, a small force in physical terms, but one which wielded influence out of all proportion to its size.

So far I have discussed the two aspects of the RAF's air defence role in Germany as if they were separate tasks, somehow discrete in organisation, command and control and execution. This was not so at all; in fact the two aspects, national and NATO, merged almost imperceptibly throughout, except for Berlin Contingency Plans under the aegis of LIVE OAK. Even here, the NATO Council of Ministers associated themselves formally with the three Allied Powers' 1954 Declaration on Berlin with an official Communique stating that any attack on Berlin would be treated as an attack upon their forces and upon themselves.[8] So integrated did the two areas become over the years that the rules for Tripartite air policing were from 1967 laid down in a NATO document (SACEUR's Rules of Engagement), a somewhat paradoxical situation formally acknowledged by the Bonn Government in 1970.[9] As we have seen, in NATO's 2ATAF area, C-in-C RAFG was also COM2ATAF, COMSOCONE an RAF officer was a NATO appointment, and the RAF air defence units performed two functions simultaneously, being the UK's contribution to the integrated air defence of the Central Region while at the same time carrying out the UK's tripartite air policing responsibilities and ensuring air access to Berlin; for example, the fighter squadrons formed the RAF Battle Flight at one and the same time as contributing to SACEUR's Interceptor Alert Force. The transition from national air policing to NATO's formal alert states was seamless, with opcon of the Battle Flight returned to the UK/US in Phase Alpha (peacetime), reassumed by SACEUR at Phase Bravo (Simple or Reinforced Alert) and immediately delegated to COM2ATAF/ COMAAFCE, the same two officers as previously, but wearing different hats.

The best example of this complex system in action for real occurred in 1990, when an unidentified track emanating from the GDR/Polish border area flew direct across the Inner German Border into FRG airspace. COMSOCONE scrambled 2 USAFE F-15s from Soesterberg in Holland, being closer to the track than the RAF F-4s at Wildenrath. These intercepted the aircraft, identified it as a MiG-23, and when ordered to intervene discovered that the aircraft was pilotless. The MiG-23, presumably on auto-pilot, continued across the FRG, flew into Dutch airspace and thence into Belgian airspace, where it ran out of fuel and crashed. Meantime COMSOCONE had authorised the F-15 pilots to engage should they consider the MiG to pose a hazard to life and property.

As you can imagine, this little incident caused some considerable flurry in a number of dovecotes. The Dutch Government wanted to know why the Dutch aircraft at Soesterberg had not been scrambled and why the Dutch authorities had not been involved in the decision making, particularly where authority to engage over Dutch territory was concerned. The Belgian Government asked similar questions, being not unnaturally concerned that a Warsaw Pact aircraft had crashed on their territory without their authorities being involved or consulted. In both cases the military chiefs understood the situation, but were extremely hard pressed to convince their political masters that the incident had been handled exactly in accordance with governing procedures and rules of engagement, with COMSOCONE acting initially in a tripartite role before metaphorically swapping his RAF hat for his NATO hat as the MiG left FRG airspace and crossed into Holland. As an immediate consequence, the Dutch authorities increased the readiness state of their Quick Reaction Alert aircraft to cover incidents over their own national territory. Nor were the lessons of the incident lost on the Germans, who at this stage were grappling with the complexities of planning for unification, including how they would take over responsibility for their own air defence for the first time since 1945. This issue, which should have been relatively straightforward to resolve, adopting the NATO model over the former territory of the FRG with a national structure over the former GDR, in fact turned out to be hard fought and contentious. The Germans, conscious of their new found sovereignty and busy establishing a national command structure, were reluctant to hand over the responsibility to NATO and initially toyed with the idea of going it alone and assuming responsibility for all aspects of air defence over the total territory of the unified country. When they accepted that this would undermine the integrated nature of NATO air defence, they insisted on retaining the right to authorise engagement over German territory, initially at no less than Chancellor level. Eventually a compromise was reached in which it was agreed that they would be consulted through their appointed duty officer in any decision to engage over former FRG territory with a right to veto. The situation was subsequently normalised into the establishment of a CAOC at Kalkar under German Command. As you can see from this saga, sovereignty over national airspace is an important and sensitive issue, which makes the RAF's tenure of it Germany for so many years all the more remarkable.

In conclusion, then, from a historical perspective, what were the determinants driving the RAF's air defence posture in Germany, and what were our achievements? Interestingly, the determinants were not those one would traditionally associate with air defence, i.e. the threat and geography. Only inasmuch as one was conscious of a hostile power the other side of the IGB, who had massive resources and who, if he chose to attack, would do so en masse. Was the threat a driver? Rather, politics was the major determinant of our air defence presence in Germany; the politics inseparable from our Quadripartite Rights and Responsibilities for Germany as a whole from which came our tripartite air policing responsibilities and our role in ensuring air access to Berlin; and the politics inherent in membership of the NATO Alliance, and our desire to respond positively to NATO Force Goals.

Finance, particularly foreign exchange costs, was the second major determinant, being the driving force behind those who over the decades argued that we should abandon our air defence role in Germany, and when those arguments were each time refuted for political reasons, drove us to adopt the minimalist air defence posture I have described realising maximum value in money and effort.

As for achievements, I believe these were considerable. To hold aircraft at the highest states of alert uninterrupted for nigh on 45 years is not insignificant in terms of organisation and commitment. The leading role we consistently played in developing and updating concepts of operation and in the many multinational training exercises was also of major value to NATO. But far more important was the influence our air defence presence allowed us to wield in both political and military circles. A pervasive theme of this paper has been that the influence we were able to exert was out of all proportion to the scale of air defence resources we were prepared to commit. Perhaps another achievement worth recording with the benefit of historical hindsight is that, despite the anomalous air policing situation that I have described and the somewhat tenuous legal basis for it after 1954, we managed the issue – air incidents et al, of which there were many – in a way which did not provoke the increasingly powerful West Germany to seek to regain the sovereignty over her own airspace which she could rightfully have claimed. That was, I suggest, an achievement of considerable political importance.

Footnotes
1   *Defending Northern Skies 1915-1995.* RAF Historical Society 1996.
2   MC 54/1.
3   Defence Council Meeting 31 Jul 1962, D(62)12.
4   a) Joint Four Power Declaration on Maintenance of Rights and Responsibilities in

Germany, published 9 Nov 1972.

b) Quadripartite Agreement signed at Berlin 3 September 1971.

5   Convention on the Settlement of Matters Arising out of the War and Occupation, Chapter 12, Civil Aviation, Article 6.

6   Source: HQ RAFG Documents.

7   ACAS(P) 9676 dated 18 March 1948.

8   Communique on Berlin issued by the North Atlantic Council, 16 December 1958.

9   Agreement between the Federal Ministers of Transport and Defence on the coordination of areas of interest between Air Navigation Services, Civil Aviation, and Air Defence in peacetime.

4. Defensive Operations

Air Marshal Ian Macfadyen CB OBE

Air Marshal Ian Macfadyen has over 5,000 flying hours including operational tours on the Lightning at Gütersloh and the Phantom. Among many staff appointments he has been PSO to the Commander 2ATAF and the C-in-C RAF Germany. He has recently retired after four years as Director General of the Saudi Armed Forces Project (Al Yamamah).

You have heard the background to the RAF's role in air defence in Northern Europe, and of the particular part the RAF, along with the Americans and French, were asked to play. I want, in our historical survey, to examine how the theory was put into practice, although time constraints limit how much I can speak of operations and training.

Going back to BAFO, in 1945, it is hard, from this distance in time, to imagine the scenario of a wrecked Germany and of RAF personnel eager to get back home to their civilian jobs.

It is perhaps less hard to imagine a mighty Russia, seemingly determined to wreak revenge on the whole of Germany. The air defence of the region, and the policing of the airspace over what was then the northern half of occupied Germany, including, in the policing case, the Berlin air corridors set up in 1946, was initially left to the remnants of the aircraft that had swept across Europe in support of the allied armies. The British contribution to the Potsdam Agreement was to provide aircraft at two or five minutes readiness to cover these tasks. As you have heard, this became known as the National Battle Flight. The actual area to cover included Holland, Belgium and part of Denmark. The RAF's Tempests and Spitfires then in service were left to do the job. It was a time when large numbers (around 650) of our fighters were based well forward near to the inter-German border.

It was an age too when we were confident of flying fighter aircraft up the air corridors to Berlin and landing at Gatow for a detachment period. A picture, showing Tempests flying over Berlin, serves to demonstrate that we took our rights seriously and exercised them accordingly, although such provocation often generated a reaction from the Soviets. Such detachments, I should add, also sometimes alarmed West Berliners. Night flying by fighters over Berlin did cause some consternation amongst people who had been so used to such things during the war when the result was usually a heavy air raid. The dramatic reduction in fighter numbers, between 1945 and 1947, (from around 650 to 150), along with similar reductions elsewhere in the air and on the ground, combined with the fact that the Soviet Union were continuing to keep forces in Eastern Europe as if WWII had not ended, led eventually, as we have heard, to the confrontation over Berlin.

During the Berlin airlift operation, most fighter squadrons had to be moved back to allow room for the myriad of transport aircraft. By now, an ADIZ had been set up to prevent the frequent unintentional allied incursions into Eastern Europe. With the crude navigational devices of the day, it was not surprising that such errors were common. Inadequate radar cover only added to the problem. This had led to frequent scrambles - often seeking allied aircraft that had strayed into East Germany. Subsequently, with the Berlin Airlift over, it was decided not to routinely enforce our flying rights to and from Berlin with fighters, but rather with transport and communications aircraft. Instead, as Sir Roger Palin has told us, Tripartite contingency plans for such operations were drawn up, involving the fighter escort of unarmed aircraft, and practised regularly in exercises over West Germany. These exercises continued until the late 1980s.

The Tempests and Spitfires of 1945 were short-lived and were replaced within two years by the Vampire FB5 - a nice aeroplane to fly and one that brought air defence in BAFO into the jet age. Both the Tempest and the Vampire retained an Air/Ground capability along with daylight air defence - something that reminds us there is nothing new about multi-roling. These skills were practised on a number of ranges then in Germany, including the base at the famous beach resort of Sylt - a name that is still a trigger for many a story amongst the more senior in years here today.

The experience of the Korean War saw the next step-change in capability and in numbers.

Indeed, numbers quickly doubled before building up further in the first half of the 1950s. The Soviet Union had brought into service their MiG-15 in Korea, and had proved in combat just how effective this aircraft could be, especially at high altitude. The Vampire was no match for the MiG which had also begun to deploy to Soviet Forces in Eastern Europe, and yet the Swift and Hunter were experiencing delays coming into service. The US MDAP came to our rescue, and in 1952, 2TAF, as it was known by then, began to receive the Sabre F-4 - a Canadian-built version of this famous aircraft. An "ad hoc" OCU was set up at the brand-new base at Wildenrath and several squadrons quickly formed. The excellent Sabre provided the backbone of air defence in 2TAF until 1956.

The introduction of the Sabre turned out to be a wise move as the Swift became a spectacular failure and the Hunter therefore had to meet all RAF requirements. The Hunter eventually began entering service in 2TAF in 1955, and it was to become the principal day fighter in the Command for the next seven years.

The announcement of the infamous Duncan Sandys Defence White Paper of 1957 was the backdrop to a dramatic run-down in 2TAF later in that year. 9 Hunter and 6 Vampire Squadrons were disbanded in just 9 months (and that was in 2TAF alone!) The remnants of about 60 fighters carried on, with a further large reduction in numbers in 1960 until the last AD Hunter Squadron disbanded in 1962.

Thus far I have ignored the question of the all-weather fighter force, so let me go back briefly to 1945. Initially, as Sir Roger briefly mentioned, no night fighter squadrons were based in the BAFO Command, the aim being to deploy NF Mosquitoes from Fighter Command should this prove necessary. With the build-up associated with the tension over the Korean War, Meteor NF11s, 12s and 14s were introduced in the early 50s, but these were no real match for the opposition. The introduction of the delta wing Javelin in the autumn of 1957 brought a welcome improvement in capability - but even this was at a time when the Americans were introducing the supersonic F-102 into their inventory (a situation not without its parallels in more recent history). It should be remembered that the early marks of Javelin were, like their predecessors, only gun-armed (although admittedly four 30mm Aden guns brought considerable short-range firepower). It was not until the Javelin FAW9 came into service, in what had now become RAF Germany, in 1959, with its additional armament of 4 Firestreak AAMs, that a significant improvement in capability occurred. Firestreak was an infra-red heat-seeking missile; it had a limited rear sector envelope and then only in clear visibility; but it did bring a welcome boost to more effective air defence. By 1962 all that remained to carry out the RAF's air defence duties was 2 squadrons of Javelins, based well back at RAF Geilenkirchen, which between them carried on the Battle Flight duties of two aircraft at a constant RS05. This state of readiness, quite a drain on just two squadrons, was to continue until Battle Flight was wound up, as I shall explain later.

By the early 1960s Soviet superiority was very real, with Brewer bombers and MiG-21 fighters leading the Soviet Air Force tactical capabilities. By this time the NATO missile defence belt was being set up, with Hawk batteries providing low-level air defence up near the inter German border, and with the medium level Nike belt behind. Fighter aircraft were now tasked to operate behind these SAM belts or under the HIMEZ, as this accorded with SACEUR's policy of defence in depth, and the desire to have air bases well to the rear, where they presented a more difficult target to the Warsaw Pact air forces. The Lightning had begun to enter the RAF inventory in 1960, but the F1 was a crude version by later standards with VHF radios and a very short range. It did have real performance, however, being capable of speeds of up to Mach 2, and of intercepting targets at 60,000 feet or more. It had long been expected the Lightning would deploy to RAF Germany to replace the Javelin, but the longer range version was slow to enter service and so the improved F2, of which there were conveniently only two squadrons, was selected to move. The first such squadron deployed in September 1965 - I recall it well, as I was one of those to deploy. It was well recognised that an aircraft with an endurance of, at best, 1 hr 10 mins was very limited in what it could do, especially if it had to enforce the integrity of the Berlin Air Corridors. This was recognised, but it was felt of critical importance that the Lightning should deploy to Germany, as we were getting seriously out of balance with our US counterparts. Besides, the Javelin had severe fatigue problems and could not long continue in service. I think the Javelin was probably the only British fighter to have the limitation of not being permitted to be looped!

RAF Gütersloh was the chosen base for the Lightning, partly

because Geilenkirchen, the Javelin base, was scheduled to be closed as an economy measure, but also because it was relatively well forward where the limited range of the F2 could be used to best advantage. It was recognised this was not in accordance with the doctrine of rearward based air defence but the Lightning's limited range proved to be the deciding factor. Even then, operating from Gütersloh, the F2 could only fly escort up to Berlin at 10,000 feet (the top of the corridor height) in the central corridor, and then fly back out at 36,000 feet - with no allowance for combat. So, for Berlin contingency operations, the aircraft had to deploy even further forward to one of the original post-war fighter bases, Fassberg, which was by then a Luftwaffe unit and inside the ADIZ. 92 Squadron joined 19 in Germany in early 1966, but for 15 months had to be based at Geilenkirchen because there was insufficient space at Gütersloh. This made the mounting of Battle Flight at Gütersloh even more complex.

The decision to modify the Lightning F2, principally to extend its range, had been made before the deployment to Germany; the modification was to the equivalent of the F6 standard. This included a much larger under-fuselage fuel tank. This became know as the F2A, and it entered service in March 1968. Many regard this version of the Lightning as the best of them all; it retained the Aden gun capability (which was not included in the F6) and it proved to have an excellent safety record .

By the mid 1960s the new NATO doctrine, known as MC14/3, had been introduced. This urged NATO forces to fight a conventional war for as long as possible. Implementation of this policy led to a radical re-equipment of RAF Germany in the 1970s, and a far greater emphasis on low-level operations. It had long been the intention of the RAF to place the Phantom in the air defence role as soon as sufficient Jaguar aircraft were around to take over the Phantom's previous reconnaissance/ground attack work. The final stage of this extensive re-equipment programme was the replacement of the Lightning F2As by the Phantom. During the changeover period, the opportunity was taken to base the Phantoms further back at Wildenrath where all operations could be carried out behind and below the HIMEZ (unlike at Gütersloh where the HIMEZ had to be penetrated to and from CAP), and at the same time move the army support Harrier force forward to Gütersloh.

Unlike the Lightning, the Phantom had excellent range. The risks of Soviet border incursions were considered relatively low (and this proved to be the case), and rearward basing was, in any event, in accordance with SACEUR's wish for defence in depth, as I have explained. The Phantom, introduced in 1977, brought with it another great leap forward in air defence capability. It was equipped with a pulse-doppler radar, four Sparrow all aspect radar-guided missiles which gave it a true all weather capability, and also 4 IR missiles, initially the AIM-9G Sidewinder but later the advanced all aspect AIM-9. This gave the Phantom four times the capability of the Lighting in numbers of AAMs but also weapons of far greater effect, let alone the ability, for the first time, to detect low-level targets at long range.

With such a capable aircraft it is no surprise that the Phantom remained in the Command until the dramatic events in the Soviet Union at the end of the 1980s saw the reunification of Germany. One consequence was that the need to police West German airspace on a tripartite basis ceased. Battle Flight operations, begun after WWII in 1945 were gradually wound down, with the UK and USA alternately sharing the 2ATAF area commitment, before they finally ended in 1991. As part of the run down of the RAF, the Phantom was subsequently withdrawn from RAF Germany, and indeed from the RAF at large.

So ended an important era of RAF fighter operations, after 46 years. It had begun in the chaos prevailing in Europe at the end of the Second World War, and ended when Germany was, once again, reunified and an economic powerhouse.

5. Ground Based Air Defence

Wing Commander J G Evans MBE

After graduating from York University in 1976, Wg Cdr Gareth Evans joined the RAF Regiment. He has served on field and Rapier Sqns in the UK and Germany, and his operational tours also include Belize and Northern Ireland. His last appointment in Germany was OC the Tactical Survive-to-Operate HQ at RAF Laarbruch and is now serving with the Joint Services Command and Staff College.

The development of ground based air defence for the RAF since the end of World War 2 has been influenced more by politics and changing strategies as technological achievements. The battle for the air between 1939 and 45 proved that fighters, radar and ground based weapons were needed to control the air and that it was vital to keep abreast of threats and technological potential to maintain a lead. I will argue over the next 15 minutes or so that the UK has failed to do this but others, such as the US, Germans, French and Dutch have. Our perhaps over-concentration on fighters and radar over the past 50 years has now exposed a capability gap readily exploitable by potential enemies and despite incredible breakthroughs in missiles and directed energy weapons we, the RAF, have come to rely on fighters and short range anti-aircraft systems effective only against aircraft and air breathing systems. Consequently although we may hope to enjoy supremacy in the air when we are operating within coalition forces, the UK generally, and RAF in particular when tied to large, static deployment bases in unstable regions, is extremely vulnerable to the very real and proliferating threats posed by "rogue states" equipped with ballistic missiles tipped with biological and chemical weapons.

You may ask what this has to do with RAF Germany since 1945, but as the RAF Regiment has been the principal provider of RAF ground based air defence in Germany for the last 50 years, the degree to which the Regiment has been in favour and the extent to which war in Germany has been at the forefront of defence planning has largely determined the ability of the RAF on the ground to defend itself from the air. Consequently it is apposite that I as a Rock should recount how RAF ground based air defence has developed and that this story is set within a post-war Germany context. In describing how the RAF, and particularly the RAF in Germany, has made the transition from guns to missiles over the past 50 years I will use as sub-plots, various operations as illustrations. The story is based chronologically and with a few brief excursions is inevitably a meander through rock-ape history, but the underlying thesis is that we have short changed ourselves by failing to develop adequate defences to counter the new missile threats and may find that this comes back to haunt us.

At the end of the second World War there were 74 RAF Regiment squadrons in NW Europe deployed throughout the British Zone. Of these, 28 were assigned as Light Anti-Aircraft (LAA) squadrons for local air defence of airfields and facilities and equipped with 20mm Hispano Suiza cannon and the Bofors 40mm L 40/60 gun. As the post-war situation stabilised many of these LAA squadrons were disbanded with the remainder retained as part of the British Forces of Occupation. The years from 1947-52 saw a further re-organisation with increasing East-West tensions and the onset of the Cold War the main drivers for change. Korea and the formation of NATO were catalysts for the reformation of many of the old squadron number plates and the growing threat from manned Soviet bombers accentuated the development of an Air Defence organisation within Germany. A total of 20 RAF Regiment LAA squadrons and 10 Wing HQs (together with 6 armoured car and rifle squadrons) were assigned to 2nd Tactical Air Force and many of these were also used in support of RAF operations in Palestine, Kenya and Malaya.

In the mid-50s to early 60s the RAF Regiment LAA force in Germany had mixed fortunes. On the one hand, in 1955 the 18 LAA squadrons were re-equipped with the Bofors 40mm L40/70 gun, a significant improvement over its predecessor as it was electrically powered and radar controlled, but the Sandys Defence paper of 1957 resulted in a fundamental reassessment of defence needs. As it envisaged trip-wire response, first use nuclear weapons in Germany and the demise of manned aircraft in favour of the ballistic missile, the requirement for air defence in Germany largely disappeared and consequently many of the RAF Regiment LAA squadrons disbanded, re-roled to field, redeployed to the UK or relocated to meet operational needs in the Middle and Far East.

However the American involvement in Vietnam in the mid-60s proved that air-bases remained vulnerable and needed intimate defence from both air and ground attack, and the threat to the air force when on the ground was rammed home in the 1967 Arab-Israeli war when the Israelis caught most of the Egyptian Air Force on the ground and, virtually unhindered, destroyed it. This, together with the realisation that the manned aircraft would not be rendered obsolete soon and the emergence of a NATO strategy of flexible response in Europe, forced reassessment of defence planning. The late 60's saw the beginning of the NATO hardening programme with bases turned into fortresses, and aircraft and assets dispersed and protected within hardened concrete structures. Once again air defence became fashionable and NATO hastened the development of an integrated air defence system in Europe based on a mix of guns, missiles and fighters. The US and other European nations fielded SAM systems such as the Nike Hercules with a range of in excess of 140 kms, command guidance, 2 stage solid propellant motor and dual nuclear/HE tipped warhead. These were later supplemented by the "Homing all the Way Killer" or Hawk missile system, an extremely capable, mobile, semi-active homer with a ceiling in excess of 11,000 metres. Supported by long range radars these SAMs were arranged in belts across Germany and in clusters of missile engagement zones or MEZs for more local defence, and it was anticipated that they would take a heavy toll of enemy aircraft fighting through to targets located in the middle and rear of the country.

The principal British SAM in the 60s was Bloodhound Mk 1 and this was deployed by the RAF within the UK with the Army weapon, Thunderbird, available both at home and on the Continent. However, in the latter part of the decade work started on upgrading this system and also on developing a shorter range but more mobile and flexible missile capability. As an interim measure the lightweight naval Seacat missile was adapted for land operations and renamed Tigercat. Uniquely, one squadron of the RAF Regiment was equipped in 1970 with this daylight-only, command-linked weapon and it was earmarked for a Germany reinforcement role. However, of more significance it was also intended to be a lead into Rapier, the new air defence missile system under development, and give the Regiment experience in missile operations. Recognising the dearth of ground based air defence in Germany and keen to qualify for NATO funding to meet its hardening programme, the RAF deployed two Regiment Bofors squadrons to Laarbruch and Gütersloh for the, now renamed Low-Level Air Defence (LLAD) role, and additionally on 1 Jan 1971, 25 Squadron (RAF) was equipped with Bloodhound Mk 2 and deployed to Brüggen with flights located at Laarbruch and Wildenrath to reinforce the NATO SAM belts and provide MEZ cover over the clutch airfields. Bloodhound's semi-active homing missile system used local surveillance radar for early warning and a target illuminating radar for guidance and was driven by ramjet and solid propellant giving it a range in excess of 80 kms. 25 Sqn was to operate Bloodhound in Germany until March '83 and was the only non-Regiment, RAF ground-based air defence weapon system in Germany in the post-war period.

The American and Egyptian experience of the vulnerability of air on the ground, together with an acknowledged weakness in anti-aircraft cover led the RAF - and other NATO nations - to adopt other non-active measures to counter the manned aircraft threat. The development of passive defences to mitigate the effects of enemy air attack included the fortification and hardening programmes and was a notable feature of the 70's. All who were in Germany at this time will remember days spent in NBC suits, early morning call-outs and the attention paid to contamination control and sheltering, dispersal, decoys, camouflage and revetting. Almost inevitable, the Brits tended to the "Blue Peter" approach of relying on flexibility, enthusiasm, creativity, sticky-backed plastic, string and sandbags on overcoming the problem of protecting airfields whereas others seemed to pump money and concrete into their solution. Passive defence although not sexy, was and still is an important element in defence planning and preparation, and required guile, hard work and some relatively sophisticated approaches. TACEVAL exposed all NATO nations' strengths and weaknesses and although the British way sometimes appeared a little ad hoc, the RAF were consistently proved to be expert practitioners and innovative leaders in this black art. This was just as well because our active ground based air defences were relatively weak and only began to improve significantly with the build up of the Rapier force.

The 70s were dominated in RAF ground based air defence terms by the development of Rapier and in 1972 the Air Force Board agreed to form six Rapier-equipped RAF Regiment squadrons based in the UK and Germany. 63 Sqn RAF Regiment formed as the joint RAF/Army trials unit at Gutersloh and HQ 4 Wg, which was to control Rapier in Germany, formed at Brüggen, later to move to Wildenrath. Following the development of Rapier standard A, a daylight-only system equipped with a surveillance radar and range of some 6 kms, RAF Regiment Rapier squadrons were formed at the remaining three Germany bases in 1976 thereby providing air defence cover for all RAFG bases. In 1978 the introduction of Blindfire radar trackers to the Germany squadrons gave Rapier an all weather, day/night capability and the first operational test for this "B Standard" upgrade was provided later that year when Germany Rapier squadrons took over on a roulement basis from the now disbanding Bofors and Tigercat squadrons, the responsibility for the air defence of Belize alongside their Harrier colleagues from Germany and the UK.

RAF Rapier went to war first in 1982 with the invasion of the Falkland Islands by Argentina. 63 Sqn RAF Regiment from Gütersloh deployed with 8 Blindfire Rapier fire units on the QE2 and landed at San Carlos. It supported the yomp across the islands, provided air defence for the Harrier strip constructed at San Carlos and eventually ended up at Stanley and provided Short Range Air Defence (SHORAD), the new buzz word, for the airfield there.

This started a long association between the RAF Regiment and the Falklands and Rapier squadrons have provided air defence cover continuously since the war, first at Stanley and later at the new airfield at Mount Pleasant. RAF Germany based squadrons were, and continue to be at the forefront of this commitment and the roulement continues. However, the Falklands conflict was an aside from the important task of deterrence in NW Europe and the decade was marked by the development of an increasingly capable NATO air defence organisation and considerable multinational training within Germany. Within a layered defensive screen, Rapier systems provided localised SHORAD for RAF airfields which were in turn protected by the longer legged SAMs and finally fighters. However, whereas other nations, both East and West, were developing and introducing extremely capable new SAM systems such as the soon to become famous Patriot, we - both the RAF and Army - fielded only short range systems with the withdrawal of Bloodhound, and relied on others for medium and long range SAM support.

As an historical aside and further evidence of the British ability to adapt and improvise, some improvements to the RAF's air defence inventory came from captured Argentine 35mm double-barrelled Oerlikon guns and Skyguard radar control systems which were refurbished and allocated to two specially formed Royal Auxiliary Air Force Regiment squadrons. These impressive systems had claimed at least one Harrier during the conflict and the Auxiliary squadrons were given a Germany reinforcement role - despite demands from Oerlikon to the UK for the settlement of unpaid Argentinean bills - and for a short time before the demise of Bloodhound, the RAF possessed the ideal fighter, Sam and gun mix. Nevertheless, the UK trend was for short range missile systems and although the new Rapier 2000 systems, or Field Standard C, was under development and promised much, the limitations of British ground based air defence came to be exposed most obviously in 1990 with the onset of the Gulf war.

26 Sqn RAF Regiment from Laarbruch and two other UK based Rapier Squadrons equipped with upgraded B Standard systems, together with 2 RAF Regiment Wing HQs to co-ordinate and control national and coalition base defences and a Germany-based field squadron for ground defence, were deployed to Saudi Arabia and Bahrein. The Rapier squadrons were integrated into the coalition layered air defence organisation and gave an excellent account of themselves but Rapier was not challenged by manned aircraft and could not counter the real air threat of Scud ballistic missiles. The need for protection against these politically and militarily significant weapons was one of the real lessons to emerge from the war and although Patriot enjoyed high profile successes it had its limitations and subsequently various international programmes emerged to develop a deployable anti-ballistic missile capability and even the UK, for a short time, set up a Medium SAM project team.

The 90's have been characterised, like the 50's, by extensive change and re-organisation in the wake of a collapsed Soviet Union and Warsaw Pact. 'Options for Change' and the Defence Costs study resulted in the decision for the RAF to withdraw from Germany by stages and this inevitably affected the RAF Regiment Rapier squadrons. The Oerlikon squadrons were disbanded, 63 Squadron on the closure of Gütersloh disbanded but the number plate was adopted by the Queens Colour Squadron; 16 Squadron was for a short time placed in a reserve category on the closure of Wildenrath but reformed as a Rapier squadron and relocated to Honington; 26 Squadron at Laarbruch moved last month with its Rapiers to Waddington and 37 Squadron will redeploy in a couple of years to an as yet unspecified location in the UK. When these moves are complete the story of ground based air defence in Germany will be over but the 90's have also seen other important developments, some good and some bad. Rapier standard B has been replaced by Rapier 2000 and this excellent system with more missiles, better radars, superb reliability, an electro-optical secondary guidance system and the ability to defeat cruise missiles will be the mainstay of the 4 squadron RAF Regiment Rapier force for many years to come. This force is an important element of the new UK immediate reaction force or IRF which is required to deploy rapidly to almost anywhere in the world and this new operational concept which stresses jointery and combined international operations is the lifeblood of this college. RAF ground based air defence is therefore at the heart of the UK's current war fighting and peace keeping efforts but the MSAM project has been put firmly on the backburner and the UK will continue to rely on others for low-level gun and long range missile systems for air and anti-missile defence. Passive defence has once again become an extremely important element of our defensive arrangements with NBC protection almost the first consideration during deployment planning, swiftly followed by the availability of filtered shelters and biological and chemical detectors, dispersal and physical protection of air assets, and arrangements to ensure redundancy through secondary operating capabilities.

A variety of systems are under development by countries either individually or in consortia, to counter the missile threat and meet the new challenges posed by deployed operations. The US is developing advanced PAC 3 versions of Patriot, a new deployable and highly capable system called ERINT and is conducting considerable research and testing on a high altitude Theatre Air Defence or THAAD system. Russia has the SA 12 available now and this system, a Patriot look-a-like, has both anti-air and anti-missile capability.

Meanwhile France and Israel are also developing new dual capable missile systems. On the other hand, the UK has decided to forgo a medium range capability and has only lukewarm interest in ballistic missile defence and prefers to rely on others for a protective umbrella over deployed forces. Unfortunately we can never be sure that they will come to the party until the music starts.

My story is coming to the end and I have no wish to end on a gloomy note or be accused of special pleading. The RAF in Germany through almost exclusively the RAF Regiment efficiently and effectively made the transition from simple gun systems to advanced short range missile systems. We are admired as excellent air defence practitioners and Rapier 2000 is acknowledged as world beating against aircraft and cruise missiles. However although we can expect to enjoy superiority in the air, especially perhaps with Eurofighter, the real air threat nowadays to our deployed forces is from missile attack and we, the RAF, cannot actively counter this. This capability gap needs to be rectified if we are going to continue to operate in high threat areas, and the signs are that we will. The fortunes of RAF anti-air from the ground have reflected closely the fortunes of my Branch and its role in Germany and we have much to be proud of. I suppose therefore my end of term report as Germany closes should be "Made great strides, needs to take giant leaps".

6. *Morning Discussion*

ACM Sir Michael Armitage: Could I ask you to plug two gaps, one of them concerns LIVE OAK, which had, I believe, a maritime, as well as land and air dimensions. Could someone explain exactly what it was and who commanded it. Secondly, both the Soviets and the Western Allies recognised, in the tensions over Berlin, the need to avoid a cock-up, and this led to the formation of the Berlin Air Safety Centre. Perhaps someone could tell us about that.

ACM Sir Roger Palin: In practical terms, although it was not strictly within NATO's territory, Berlin could not be divorced from NATO. So, LIVE OAK was set up as a tripartite organisation with its command post, JACK PINE, alongside the SHAPE headquarters complex. This all started under General Norstadt when Berlin was the focus of East/West confrontation - at a time when there was nothing between an incident on the border - or in the corridor - and total nuclear war. LIVE OAK's function was to develop contingency plans providing a series of graded responses to potential incidents affecting access to the city. Some of these were exercised. For example, on the air defence side, each year we would put up elements of British, US and French fighter squadrons in mixed formations to practise one of these operations. Typically, you would send a military transport down the corridor unescorted to see what the other side did, or you might escort it down and observe the reaction; there was a series of other options.

There was a maritime dimension to all of this, both in terms of our own national plans and through COMTWOATAF, from which the Royal Air Force in Germany could not be divorced. As part of SACEUR's Air Defence Force, COMTWOATAF's responsibilities were actually wider than C-in-C RAFG's, in terms of national air policing, because COMTWOATAF had air defence commitments over the Baltic and up to the Danish border, whereas the air policing responsibilities under the National hat were very much restricted to the Federal Republic of Germany's air space.

Air Cdre Phil Wilkinson: The Berlin Air Safety Centre - the BASC - was part of the immediate post-war four-power arrangement. It established a Control Zone, based on the geographical centre of Berlin, with a radius of (at Field Marshal Montgomery's insistence) 20 statute miles. Uniquely, it continued to function as a four-power authority until the day of German unification. All aircraft entering any of the corridors en route to Berlin would have their flights co-ordinated by the BASC, the Russians allocating each flight a level of clearance, either 'fully safe', 'maybe safe' or 'recommended you don't try it'. In the early days there were several unfortunate incidents when 'trying it' did bring effective reaction from the Russians and aircraft were lost in the corridor. Interestingly enough, during the Airlift itself the centre remained alive and kicking and the Russians were actively engaged in monitoring, controlling and making sure the Airlift was a 100% success!

On the day that German airspace eventually became sovereign, everybody who had never been allowed to do so before wanted to fly into Berlin - which caused chaos. The procedures were rapidly reshaped under the guidance and leadership of the RAF representative at the BASC, Wg Cdr Peter Donman, who became such a pivotal figure in the transitional period that he stayed on as a Senior Consultant and managed German air traffic control over Berlin and the former GDR until about a year and half ago.

AVM Michael Robinson: Did the squadrons have an annual training commitment to fire weapons?

AM Ian Macfadyen: Yes, we did. As I recall it was an allocation of about four or five missiles per squadron per year, which meant that, on average, each pilot would fire one live missile during his tour. It might be a telemetry round, or, like the one that I had the privilege of firing, a live missile with a warhead, leading to spectacular results with a direct hit on the flare. The training was very much at medium to high level in my day; it went lower later, with the Jindivik being used to tow a flare to test the heat-seeking element.

ACM Sir Andrew Wilson: I would add that, in addition to what the air defence squadrons were doing, all the Phantom operators, ground attack and recce, used to go to Valley and fire Sidewinder against the Jindivik, but I don't think many of the squadrons actually fired any other types of missile.

Sir Roger Palin: As far as guns were concerned, in the old days, the Hunters went up to Sylt and we reintroduced APCs at Decimomannu on an annual basis from about 1970/71, but only when we got the Lightning 2A with its integral guns. Prior to that, one just exercised the guns by firing them over the North Sea to make sure they worked.

Wg Cdr Gareth Evans: Tigercats were originally fired at Aberporth and the Rapier force had a long association with the Hebrides - other squadrons always seemed to go to Crete and places like that while I always ended up in winter in the Outer Hebrides! We had about 30 missiles a year; a squadron still has broadly the same number. There are no telemetry rounds - all live missiles. We fired against Rushton targets towed by Canberras and, unlike the Air Marshal, the one missile I ever got was a dud!

Gp Capt 'Jock' Heron: In 1961, when the numbers of fighters in 2ATAF were reduced to almost zero, there was a significant rise in Russian pressure on NATO. Was that just a coincidence, or was it a lesson? - that numbers and size are important if you wish to demonstrate real political intent?

Sir Roger Palin: I would say that, so far as UK national numbers were concerned, you would be right. Fighter numbers were very low. The whole of NATO would have had more - although they were involved in a re-equipment programme. It was the Khruschev era - and there was Cuba. I think it was strategic and macro politics that actually drove things, rather than the numbers of aircraft that happened to be in RAFG's ORBAT. But there was a linkage the other way, because, although politics was the main driver for our air defence presence - rather than the threat - you can never divorce the two. One of the reasons why the Cabinet reversed its decision in 1962, and we remained in the air defence role and introduced the Lightning, was actually the developing supersonic capability of the other side, which we needed to match. I would say that capability is more important than numbers.

Gp Capt Stuart Peach: Another important factor is 'sustainability'. Some of our present forces are overstretched and, for instance, the RAF looks to roulement to sustain the Tornado GR1 force, which is committed to three concurrent operations! So, it is more than just addressing the capabilities. If you are engaged in a number of concurrent operations, as the Strategic Defence Review made clear, then it is sustaining those operations over the long term which drives the force numbers. Our problem is to get that message across, not just to the other services, but to the public at large who may well ask why we need so many Eurofighters and so on.

Wg Cdr 'Jeff' Jefford: Gp Capt Peach referred to the difference in philosophy between the British-lead 2ATAF and the US-lead 4ATAF with regard to low- or medium-level tactics and concluded that the RAFG concept was validated by the Gulf experience. It seemed to me that we went to the Gulf using 2ATAF's low-level approach and finished up using 4ATAF's medium level techniques. Would you comment on that?

Stuart Peach: As the Air Commander in the Gulf, I think Sir Andrew should answer part of that! For myself I don't think there is any reason for us to be defensive about going to war at low-level. In JP233 we had the weapon that General Schwarzkopf needed to stop the Iraqi Air Force from intervening during the first few days. At that stage of the campaign it was not given that we would rapidly establish precisely that air supremacy that would permit medium level operations - there is no doubt that it was a risk assessment exercise on the part of the Commanders to switch to medium level operations. But, unlike many American commentators, I would not conclude that their decision somehow devalued low-level tactics. I would add that, if General Mike Jackson, the current COMARRC was sat here, he would react in a very similar way. He tells an anecdote from Bosnia to the effect that the American (by now, I would argue, not far off) dogma of medium level being the only way, meant that when generals on the ground needed a show of force, they didn't get it - because operating at 15,000 feet does not show the opposition 'in your face' air power. So, I would argue that low-level tactics, low-level penetration, low-level full stop, are not dead.

Sir Andrew Wilson: I would not dispute anything that Gp Capt Peach has said, but I do agree with 'Jeff' Jefford that it was a defining moment when we had to go to medium level. We hadn't really had a lot of discussion about it - the actual decision was taken, of course, by Bill Wratten and 'Paddy' Hine after I left. There was some debate just before I handed over - but we were 'employed' by the Americans, in a word, to handle the low-level role. But I do think that, in historical terms, it was a defining moment.

Ian Macfadyen (Chief of Staff to Gen de la Billière at the time): I agree with Stuart Peach. I think we should remember that in the Gulf War the RAF brought with it the unique capability of JP233 and that it was very much welcomed by the Americans because it enabled us to attack airfields at time when we expected a large response from what was, at least on paper, a 700-strong air force. Because the opening moments blinded the Iraqis so completely that they really didn't know what was going on thereafter, we were able to dominate the airspace from the first day. It is a myth that we were shot down dropping JP233. That is absolutely not true. There is no evidence that any Tornado was shot down dropping JP233. One we're not sure about who left the target and crashed 15 miles beyond, probably not as a result of direct fire attack. I have to say that anybody who did that operation must have been suitably terrified - at night - with flak which was at least twice as dense as on any Warsaw Pact airfield. So, it was a brave thing to do. But, we caught them by surprise and once we had gained the dominance of the air, it was logical to go to medium level. It was a defining moment, as we have just heard, but the fact that we had trained at low-level - and that we were trained to be flexible - enabled us to change to medium level with remarkable ease. Now, we had all sorts of limitations about what we could do at medium level - we were dropping 1,000 pounders, for heaven's sake, in dive attacks from 20,000 feet, using pretty crude aiming devices. Eventually we brought in laser-guided bombs and started to do it more effectively.

ACM Sir Anthony Skingsley: I think we should recognise that USAFE converted quite quickly to low-level. If you go back to 1974, when I was commanding Laarbruch and the first COMAAFCE came in - he was a medium level man - there was a big conference at Ramstein. Two USAF officers gave us a presentation on a counter-air attack against the Warsaw Pact. They went in at low-level and the C-in-C got up and said 'What are you doing?!' They said, 'Sir, we think its the best way to survive.' They were back in the States in 48 hours! That was 1974. Two years later it was a low-level force and the philosophy in the Central Region was low-level from then on. All the F-111 forces were low-level - so it wasn't a simple, 'They're medium level. We're low-level' argument. The Americans did actually accept the arguments which were put forward by 2ATAF, lead by the Brits at that time.

Sir Andrew Wilson: I would just like to add that it wasn't that we didn't want to do medium level - we didn't have the resources to do it - particularly the electronic warfare capability, which is an absolute must if you're going to go in at medium level. But you are quite right, Sir Anthony, the Americans operated at both low-level and medium level, because they had the resources.

7. An Operations Overview

Air Chief Marshal Sir Andrew Wilson KCB AFC

During his 36 years in the RAF, Sir 'Sandy' Wilson held seven different appointments relating to RAF Germany. He flew Hunters at Gütersloh, Phantoms and Jaguars at Laarbruch always with 2 Sqn which he commanded between 1975-77. As a young officer he was ADC to the C-in-C at Rheindahlen and between 1991-93 was the last C-in-C of RAF Germany and COM2ATAF.

I would like to turn first to the size and shape of offensive forces since I believe it is important to appreciate how they changed over the period. In so doing I will not dwell on the international events that shaped those changes since they were covered in depth this morning.

In February 1945 2 TAF had a UE (Unit Establishment) of almost 1500 front line aircraft (excluding 112 AOP aircraft) in some 85 Squadrons. This included a total of 803 offensive aircraft in 43 Squadrons. By April 1948 68 Squadrons had been removed and by July '50, there were just 33 light bomber aircraft left.

Then, of course, came the build-up to Korea and the March 1952 and March 1955 figures show just how dramatic that build-up was. At its height there were a total of 274 offensive aircraft in 18 Squadrons. No sooner had the forces been built up before the 1957 Sandys cuts brought the numbers down again and by March 1958 there were only 120 offensive aircraft in 10 squadrons.

There is one further point which is not evident and that is in this period strengths generally lagged behind UEs, whereas in later periods more often than not strengths exceeded UEs. This as we all know was a ploy to save money on aircrew, fuel and spares and whilst the extra airframes were generally welcome it was often a false economy.

There were further reductions with the phasing out of the Hunter and Canberra forces during the 60's and then a gradual build-up with the introduction of the Buccaneer, Phantom and Harrier in the early 70's. This re-equipment programme was arguably the most significant in the Command's history and these numbers mask a stepped increase in performance and weapon carrying capability. The Phantom, of course was a truly multi-role aircraft and the Harrier provided unique off-base capability for direct support of 1 Br Corps.

With the arrival of the Tornado and the increase to 4 strike/attack squadrons at Brüggen as part of the build-up of NATO's nuclear forces as a lead-in to the INF negotiations. Then following the collapse of the Berlin Wall in 1989 the beginning of the final run down of the Command under the UK Government's 'Options for Change' Programme.

All these changes also illustrate some important points. The first concerns aircrew to aircraft ratios. A simple division of the total numbers by the number of squadrons reveals that the average ratio in 1945 was 2 to 1. Then after the war the ratios were reduced markedly and, for example, in March 1958 were down to 1.5 to 1. Then in more recent times this declined to 1.33 to 1 for the strike squadrons and 1.2 to 1 for others. Despite plans to retrain aircrew in a time of tension the fact was that these sort of ratios put a serious question mark over our ability to sustain day and night operations, especially from the 70's when virtually all the offensive squadrons were dual-roled.

As many will recall, such ratios have been a contentious issue for much of the period and in many cases the policy has been driven more by an understandable desire to retain squadron number plates than for operational reasons. Our 'small squadron' policy was, of course, in complete contrast to that of our USAF colleagues who retained 18 AE squadrons with crews to match - even if many of them were majors! If there is a lesson for the future here it must be that for sustained operations, especially in the modern electro-optical age, aircrew to aircraft ratios must be raised closer to the 2 to 1 figure we had at the end of the last war.

This issue was compounded by the fact that certainly in the 50's, 60's, and well into the 70's there were insufficient stockpiles of weapons to support operations at intensive rates. This was only remedied in the late 70's when NATO's stockpiling guidance was enforced and checked on TACEVALs.

Having set the scene in terms of shape and size I would now like to look at a number of aspects affecting capability; and the first concerns basing.

One of the most important characteristics of the early post-war jet aircraft was their very short range compared with the piston aircraft - especially aircraft such as the Mosquito - which they replaced. This necessitated their forward basing at such bases as Fassberg, Celle and Wunstorf where they were very vulnerable to a pre-emptive strike.

With the introduction of the Hunter and Swift it was possible to use less vulnerable airfields such as Jever, Oldenburg, Ahlhorn and Gütersloh. However, it was only with the building of the 'Clutch' airfields, with their dispersals and parallel taxiways, in the mid to late 50's that 2 TAF had a survivable basing policy. Having said that, it is worth recalling that there was a limited amount of off-base dispersal for some Squadrons as early as the 50's.

But it was not until the start of NATO's hardening programme in the early 70's that Germany based aircraft had the ability to withstand a pre-emptive attack. Interestingly, the Harrier was originally based at Wildenrath with a forward-based field war role, but moved forward to Gütersloh in 1977 to facilitate peacetime training and faster deployment.

Now a few words about operational training and doctrine since in many ways they drove overall capability levels.

After the war, training was generally Wing or Squadron based and it was not until the early 1960's that there were any formal squadron training syllabi and those which existed tended to be driven more by CFS than by operational imperatives. But during the 1970's RAF Germany developed the TACEVAL concept which, interestingly, had been tried as early as 1960 at Wildenrath and Geilenkirchen.

It was this seminal work that was later to form the basis of an ACE wide evaluation programme which had a very significant effect on both our own and NATO's operational capability. Indeed, it was TACEVAL that became the real driving force in operational training. Whereas in the 50's and 60's attention focused on no notice generation exercises with limited flying, in the 70's attention switched to a mix of no notice and 3-4 day exercises which involved whole stations. This coincided with the start of the hardened era with greater emphasis on sustainability and survivability.

In parallel, the NATO Force Goal process quite rightly concentrated on capability gaps. In the RAF's case these highlighted 'amongst others' a significant weakness in active and passive ECM capability. Having said that it is important to make the point that right from the start of NATO's TACEVAL programme RAF Germany consistently led the Central Region's league tables.

Throughout this period low flying was at the heart of both operational doctrine and operational training. This was a natural follow on from the war when 2TAF had operated at ultra low-level on ground attack and recce operations. Post-war Germany offered unrivalled low flying opportunities and the RAF became masters of this key art. Many will remember the carefree days of the 50's and 60's when one could go almost anywhere at 250ft- or below! I should add that it wasn't until the advent of radar altimeters in the 70's that we found out how high 250 ft was! However, not surprisingly, anti-low flying pressure began to build in the 70's and in late 1990 the minimum height was raised to 1000ft agl with the consequence that much of the training had to be exported to the UK and this remains the case today.

Whilst RAF and 2ATAF tactical doctrine was based almost exclusively on low-level operations this was not the case in 4ATAF to the south. The USAF's experience in Korea and Vietnam, coupled with their superior EW and fighter capability, led them to adopt a mix of low and medium level tactics. With the benefit of hindsight and the Gulf War some views on these differing doctrines may emerge in discussions.

Practice weaponry played a key part in day-to-day training especially for the strike/attack squadrons. In the early days the short-range aircraft had use of ranges close to their bases such as Bergen-Hohne but there were regular APCs at Sylt off the north Germany Coast. By the late 50s Nordhorn Range had become the focus for most Germany aircraft and most crews could fly the route into the range with their eyes shut. However in the early 70s APCs were reintroduced, this time at the NATO air-to-ground range at Decimomannu in Sardinia which was parented by RAF Germany.

But it was the start of Red Flag Exercises in the Nevada Desert for RAF Germany Squadrons in 1977 that proved to be a watershed for both operational training and operational effectiveness. With the arrival of the Tornado in 1983, training was further enhanced by the introduction of OLF and TFR training into RAF Goose Bay usually as a lead-in to Flag Exercises.

I think it is also worth mentioning competitions in this context since they became an integral part of operational training for much of the period. On the national side all strike/attack squadrons, as well as the recce squadrons with a secondary attack role, took part in the annual Salmond Trophy weapons competition. But NATO competitions such as Royal Flush and Big Click and Tactical Weapons Meets dominated the training cycle often, in my view, to the detriment of operational effectiveness at unit level.

There is no doubt that competitions had their good and bad points but in 1978 they were replaced by Tactical Meets involving both offensive and defensive aircraft with the emphasis quite rightly on operational effectiveness, particularly with the development of large attack packages backed up by AWACS, tankers and escort fighters.

My last general point concerns the way the RAF introduced new types to the theatre. Whereas other nations re-equipped squadrons, the RAF had - and incidentally still does - a policy of phasing one type out and then another in. This policy was driven, I have to say for the record, more by the needs of the Air Secretary's Branch than by the operational requirement. As a consequence the transition from one type to another took longer and a great deal of expertise was wasted or lost in the process.

As an example, when the Phantom was introduced in the recce/attack role in 1970 I was one of only two pilots who moved across from the Hunter FR Wing at Gütersloh and virtually the same happened when the Phantom was replaced by the Jaguar in 1975. If there is a lesson for the future it is that the operational needs should take priority over career and posting considerations but perhaps this is a contentious view.

Overall I am in no doubt that we can be proud of the contribution that our offensive squadrons made to the operational effectiveness of the Alliance. Whilst our aircraft were not always the match of the USAF in terms of pure capability, especially in the EW field we, nevertheless, made more than the best of what we had and this was accurately reflected in RAF Germany's TACEVAL results which were demonstrably the best in the Central Region over a long period. But that begs the question of how we would have fared if we had gone to war against the Warsaw Pact?

With the benefit of hindsight - and especially in the light of what we now know about Soviet equipment and training in those days - I think that history will judge that we would have done much better than we might have believed at the time.

8. Offensive Operations - Strike

Air Commodore P J Wilkinson CVO

After National Service as a RAF officer, Phil Wilkinson graduated from Oxford and rejoined the Service in 1961. He flew the Canberra with 14 Sqn in Germany and again with 85 Sqn, later commanding 237 OCU (Buccaneers), and is a graduate of the French Air Force College and the USAF War College. He has served at the MOD and at SHAPE; his final appointment being Defence and Air Attache in Moscow.

On 1 January 1958, No 88 Squadron's Wildenrath-based Canberra B(I)8 aircraft and their two-man crews were formally committed to the nuclear strike role, using a 'low altitude bombing system' (LABS) for the toss delivery of their US-provided Mk 7 1650-1b weapon.

The Memorandum accompanying the 1958-1959 Air Estimates noted that:

"Canberras of 2nd Tactical Air Force and Bomber Command are being given nuclear capability"

With the assumption of the nuclear role, the Squadron gave up its previously assigned tasks of reconnaissance, Army cooperation and close air support. It will come as no real surprise to today's generation, brought up on the 'management of change', to hear that as early as July 1958, the Squadron had already been re-roled for conventional shallow dive bombing. Still less a surprise will be to hear that this was all in aid of a Middle East crisis, this time following the assassination of King Faisal of Iraq. But the moment passed, and the Squadron settled to a routine of training and practice attacks that characterised the next 40 years, until, on 1 April 1998, the Operational Record Book of No 88 Squadron's successor (No 14 Squadron) notes in a single sentence that "..the WE177 weapon has been withdrawn from service and the Squadron is no longer declared in the strike role."

I can only give a brief survey of the operational and domestic

The US Mk 7 (Project E) 1650lb weapon

content of those 40 years of service in Germany. Much of what was established in the first years of the nuclear role, however, was continued in many ways almost unchanged until the completion, and I therefore feel it possible to concentrate much of my presentation on the period when I was involved - at a very junior level - in all the activities of a nuclear strike squadron with Canberras as the delivery vehicle.

In that context, I shall first cover in outline the reason for a build-up of Canberras in Germany in the mid-50s. The fundamental reason was the build-up of Canberras in the UK, where the rapid rise to 24 bomber squadrons with 10 aircraft each was causing headaches over where to put them, especially since the parallel programme of airfield upgrades to accommodate the also expanding V-Force had taken away most of the remaining options. There was a brief look at bringing up to what was known as Class 2 standard (that is to say, with a 9500 feet runway) one or other of a couple of Training Command airfields - Worksop or Full Sutton - but at the end of a very short period of briefing and Air Force Board consideration, a completely different option was offered by AMSO to CAS in March 1954, which reassured him, as the Minute of the day records, that:

"...since the runways and taxy-tracks are of the requisite LCN, we see no reason why four Canberra squadrons should not form at, say, Ahlhorn, beginning 1 April of this year."

CAS approved this interestingly flexible recommendation on 29 March; PUS gave his seal of approval on 30 March; AMSO was told to get on and fix. CAS rounded off a good week's work by directing that Cs-in-C Bomber Command and 2nd TAF should have their Directives reviewed to make it clear that these four squadrons were still part of Bomber Command, under operational control, with HQ 2nd TAF their administrative masters. The Squadrons thus remained allocated to SACEUR as part of the UK's declared light bomber force. Despite the notable speed of decision-making, the 1 April target was not quite met. The first Squadron to arrive was No 149, drawn fully-formed from the Cottesmore Wing, and planned to arrive at Gutersloh. Again, no surprise to hear that runway repairs meant that the Squadron actually arrived at the originally suggested aiming point - Ahlhorn - on 25 August 1954. They moved on to Gütersloh a couple of weeks later. The remainder of the force - formed at No 551 Wing - assembled quickly after, with the Squadrons forming in-situ:

102 on 30 October, 103 on 30 November, and 104 on 15 March 1955. Their subsequent existence was in the classical Bomber Command mode, with concentration on academic medium and high-level bombing using UK and Germany ranges leading to crew classification in the various visual and blind bombing modes, together with exercises and competitions. This pattern continued until the Squadrons' disbandment and withdrawal in August 1956.

By then the original plan for the deployment to Germany of Canberra PR and NI (night intruder) squadrons had come to fruition. The PR echelon had in fact already come into being (originally with four squadrons) before the 551 Wing disappeared. The bomber/intruder squadrons were a little further back, and their designation was changing en-route - from night intruder through intruder to simply interdictor. Thus the nomenclature of the Aircraft, the B(I)6 of No 213 Squadron and the B(I)8 of the other three.

213 was the first to form - at Ahlhorn in July 1955 - but it was not until March 1956 that they received their B(I)6 aircraft. By then, 88 was up and running at Wildenrath, and a year later - in February 1957 - its aircraft were being fed into the modification programme to install the Honeywell systems that were the core of the LABS attack system. Political and technical complications surrounded the progress to full operational status (despite the February 1958 statement noting the Canberras' capability), not least the arrangements that had to be made for physical storage areas for the US weapon, and for separate accommodation for its technical support team, and for the security force who guarded it. But by September 1959, all four squadrons were each maintaining a single aircraft on QRA (increasing to two in 1962), with a requirement to be airborne within 15 minutes of the alert. The two crews were accompanied in the wired-off compound by a USAF Alert Duty Officer (usually a Lieutenant) who provided half of the two-man concept that governed all access to and handling of the weapon. The USAF air policemen similarly provided half of the security cordon, sharing the task with RAF police, both armed.

The concept of operations was straightforward: the QRA aircraft would provide immediate response to SACEUR's call for strikes, and would be able to do that either individually or as the vanguard of a fully generated force that had benefitted from a period of alert state development allowing time for the weapon loading and crew preparation to make the whole squadron available for selective

Aircraft and weapons inside 14 Sqn hangar at Wildenrath in 1965, showing the training ballistic 1650lb 'shape' store on a trolley in front of the middle aircraft

release against targets on SACEUR's strike programme. Given the Canberra's low-level radius of action - with 24,000 lbs of fuel, the B(I)8 could cover 600 nautical miles out and back in a straight line at 420 knots (365 till the wing-tip tanks were jettisoned, or at least that is what the Pilot's Notes said) to dry tanks - the targets were almost all confined to tactical airfields in one or other of the Warsaw Pact satellite countries. The primary QRA target was the one exhaustively studied by crews in regular sessions in the Operations Wing vault - the day before a QRA duty started was a mandatory study day; other sessions were programmed in with all the other routine training requirements. The visit of the Weapons Standardisation Team from the Armament Support Unit at Wittering was a regular challenge to the memory glands. So it remained until the end of the strike role earlier this year. And of course TACEVAL, and all the lower level alert and readiness tests, kept the edge permanently sharpened. With half the squadron assigned to each of the two QRA targets, it was never less than once a fortnight that a crew had a 24-hour shift in the compound. The weekend duty, covering 48 hours, came up six or seven times a year. The junior combat-ready crews could of course expect to have the several days of the Christmas break for their personal enjoyment! But that was the ground based theory. What of the flying training for the role?

   In three years on 14 Squadron I fell just nine short of 1000 hours. The role of the Squadron was totally focused on low-level operation. Hence the vast majority of sorties were two-hour excursions around a relatively-unrestricted German airspace, including first-run attacks at the main ranges and academic practice-bomb sessions, almost invariably at Nordhorn. The other continental ranges were used - in Belgium, Netherlands, and (occasionally) France - and regular runs were made to all the UK targets, but it will be the features and time checks along the LABS run to Nordhorn target that are probably still etched on the memories of anyone who served on one of the Germany squadrons of the period. The attack was a trifle mechanical, and involved pre-computing release parameters prior to take-off, which were set by the navigator on the release computer at the rear of the aircraft before clambering aboard. In-flight adjustments were possible but only by over-riding the cues that the pilot followed to initiate the pull-up. For both the standard forward toss and the reversionary 'over-the-shoulder' attacks, the approach speed was calculated (from met data) to give an Equivalent Air Speed of 434 knots; the pull-up was triggered by picking the bomb release button at the final IP and waiting until the computer-driven timer ran down and gave the cue. On a manual ILS-type instrument the driver then gathered the horizontal needle back up to the centre and maintained the vertical needle vertical (hence the Hornchurch/Biggin Hill aptitude tests!) which meant a modest application of +3.4g. Bomb release was also signalled to the driver and the mildly aerobatic escape recovery from 4000+ feet back to the 250 feet approach height was carried out ready for another run in the academic pattern.

Proficiency in this manoeuvre was of fundamental importance, both for consistent weapon accuracy and for survival. Hence the regular detachments to better weather areas with range facilities on the doorstep, for intensive work-up of new crews and consolidation for the more experienced. Thus, in my second month in the Squadron, three crews and two aircraft left the murk of North Germany in December and worked for a five-day period at RAF Idris, 20 miles south of Tripoli, and with Tarhuna range just minutes off the end of the runway. Flying started at 0600 or asap after sunrise and was as intensive as the ramp heat and the cockpit air conditioning would allow the ground and air crew to achieve. Typical day's flying was therefore a four-bomb detail, with the first being an FRA, returning to Idris after perhaps only 25 minutes for an engines-running re-arm with four more 25lb practice bombs on the wing pylons ready for the same again. That would be repeated twice more before lunchtime. Each crew would thus drop 24 bombs a day; 70+ per crew per detachment. The third crew split; one man to the range as RSO (Range Safety Officer), the other to manage the ground activities at Idris and keep the orange juice cool for the quick turn-rounds.

Range work was usually built in to the exercise sorties flown within the overall pattern of NATO training: major ATAF-wide air defence events such as Blue Moon or Cold Fire; smaller-scale air defence exercises such as Brown Falcon over Denmark; Highwood and the smaller-scale Priory versus the UK Air Defence Region; Round Robin, later Ample Gain, to check cross-servicing facilities at other NATO bases; even Datex - for the benefit of the French; and, with due political correctness, Cloggy Emotion to exercise the Dutch Forward Air Controllers. These, and many others, remained fixed points in authorisation sheets and log books until this year for the

B(I)8 airborne in the conventional role fit

strike squadrons, and will last into the foreseeable future.

The versatility of the Canberra, and its replacements - Phantom, Jaguar, Buccaneer, and Tornado - meant inevitably that it would be asked to do more than hold alert for nuclear response and the associated training. Thus the regular reversion to conventional fit - with the 4x20mm gun pack fitted in the bomb bay and all conventional weapon options available from wing pylons and the remaining forward sector of the bomb bay. Operational actuality was regularly the cause: 59 Squadron went to British Honduras (Belize) in 1958 to discourage Guatemalan advances; 213 and 88 deployed to the Gulf in mid-1961 for an early version of the Kuwait crisis; in 1963 all RAF Germany Canberra squadrons were rotating through Kuantan in Malaya to reinforce the UK response to the Indonesian confrontation.

To remain at least semi-prepared for these short-notice excursions, all Canberra squadrons had at least one three-week detachment to (usually) Cyprus, in the conventional fit - Exercise Citrus Grove. Dive bombing was against the raft targets in Episkopi Bay; strafe was at Larnaca, against targets on the salt marsh that now supports the international airport.

The highly agreeable solution to the need for readiness for these exotic deployments was simply to practise exotic deployments: this was Exercise Lone Ranger. There was hardly a day on any of the squadrons when there was not a singleton aircraft and crew somewhere down the Southern or Extended Southern Ranger route; via Cyprus, the Gulf (Sharjah, Bahrain, Masirah, or even Djibouti), through Aden and on to Nairobi and (then) Salisbury. Return routes often staged via Tehran and then had extended low-level sectors across Iran before climbing out to overfly Turkey back into Cyprus. Sometimes, too, the last homeward stage would take in some Libyan desert low-level flying, using El Adem as a refuel/re-arming point, prior to some range runs or an attempt to find the wreck of the "Lady be Good" B-24 before climbing out on fuel minima.

In mid-1966 there had been a change of strike profile: the Mk 7 LABS weapon delivery being replaced by laydown with a US Mk 43 21001b weapon. Work-up had gone well and the CEP for strike had been radically improved from LABS scores of around 200 yards to lay down scores of 60 - 80 feet. After a short pause from QRA while ground procedures and practice weapon loading had been exercised, the Squadron resumed QRA with the new weapon on 4 November.

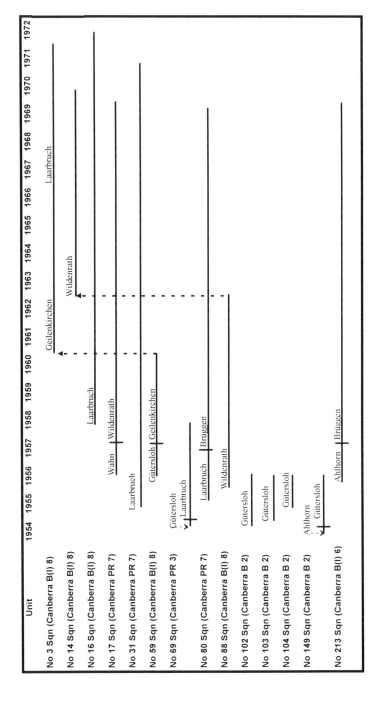

Deployment of RAF Canberras (all roles) in Germany, 1954-72

Just to prove the point, HQ RAF Germany and the Station Commander called us out for three alert and generation exercises in the next ten days. Very percipient since the NATO TACEVAL team arrived on 14 November. The Squadron received an across-the-board rating of "1" - the first for a strike unit in RAF Germany. In June 1967 the AFCENT Tactical Weapons Meet saw the Squadron just beaten by a Canadian F-104 team; the USAFE F-4Es were a long way behind. A 14 crew won the night strike competition by a wide margin. Given that the navigation equipment fit still consisted of just a steam-driven Doppler (Blue Silk) and the Decca Mk 8 (conceived a navigation system for shipping, and quite good at that sort of speed!), the abilities of the navigator fraternity were remarkable. Their working environment - in the B(I)8 - was testing to say the least: 90% of the time stretched out in the nose map-reading, contorting back at regular intervals to update the navigation equipment from the most recent visual fix. There was no ejection seat for him, just the normal entry/exit hatch and a chest parachute. My own partner was 6'1" tall and as solid as you could wish (very Irish, too). The Aviation Medicine people were concerned! But - especially if you were very small - escape was possible. On 11 June 1968 Flt Lt Stu Stringer decided to leave after his driver had had an airborne coming-together with another of the Squadron's aircraft. The driver ejected success-fully at just 200 feet, no doubt still astonished at seeing Stu roll up and dive for the ground some 800 feet earlier. All good things come to an end and - for the 18 crews still keeping 14 Squadron at full length until the last moment - on 31 May 1970 14 Squadron came off state as a Canberra strike squadron. On 1 June Wg Cdr John Sutton, with Sqn Ldr Hugh Coriat in the rear compartment, flew in the Squadron's first Phantom to its new base at Brüggen.

And the pattern remained virtually just as before. On 30 June, HQ initiated the first Exercise Quicktrain - alert reaction and, normally, weapon handling procedures. On this occasion there were neither inert weapons nor carriage equipment yet to hand. But things moved ahead quickly and in July the Weapons Standardisation Team paid their first visit. Dipping briefly into the Operations Record Book/Form 540 for the period one can see a continuation of the Canberra pattern, with generally similar aircraft to crew ratio but fewer flying hours. In January 1967 there were 13 B(I)8 Canberras for 18 crews who flew 475 hours that month. In January 1972 there were

10 F-4s for the Squadron's 15 crews but they only shared 175 hours. Those included the first Missile Practice Camp at Valley; conventional weaponry in Germany, using SUU-23 (Gatling) cannon for 34% air-to-ground scores; and also "..concentrating on strike work-up to meet RAFG requirements." As part of this the Station Commander had a 4 January MINEVAL which went through all alert and generation phases and launched six aircraft on a simulated mission profile as the conclusion of the test. Just as Canberras had disappeared to Cyprus, so their successors, but by now to the range facilities at Decimomannu.

With the excellent conventional capabilities of the F-4, much work was devoted to "..realistic profiles against missile sites" - "..large area targets typical of possible wartime targets." The advantage of having genuinely dual-capable aircraft (without the time-consuming role-change procedures) is clear. Carrying on earlier traditions the Squadron won both the overall and the dual-role trophies at the NATO Tactical Weapons Meet at Florennes in September 1972.

Yet there were always obstacles to stress-free training and programme-building. Bird-strike restrictions kept speed back to 360kts at low-level - this in October 1972. That same month saw the station run out of 41b practice bombs. The Germany weather was always a factor, and in the domestic and international political turmoil of 1973 fuel restrictions bit deep into the training task. In September 1974 they were so stringent that "..guns were removed to reduce drag."

There was as yet no real hardening of RAF Germany facilities; thus when the TACEVAL team arrived, the defensive posture was demonstrated by on-airfield dispersal into revetments. Realistic assessment of airborne performance was derived from USAFE nuclear safety and operational check crews flying chase sorties. New tactics were always readily tried: in March 1975 a radar toss delivery was being tested. But a trifle academic, since on 7 April 1975 Wing Commander Anthony Mumford flew in the first Jaguar. By the end of that month there were four. May saw the first Jaguar aircrew in strike training sessions. July 1975 found the new team literally digging in on their South-East dispersal, sandbagging and barbed-wiring their new home.

Composite working continued as Jaguar numbers increased and

F-4s dwindled. F-4 crews were still committed to QRA but the aircraft were de-roled in August. By September Jaguars were running 4-ship sorties. In October the first five nuclear-capable Jaguars were collected off the production line. On 14 November 1975 the last F-4 sortie was flown - over 14,000 sorties in the strike/attack role, with just one aircraft lost (and that to an engine fire on take-off, for his handling of which the captain was awarded a Queen's Commendation). Later that month, the still new Jaguar team wins the RAF Germany Salmond Trophy, but reverts to routine with a total of four days on MINEVAL, gaining "..valuable training during loading and acceptance of the 600/950 HE MC (training) weapons." Also the strike training rig and weapon simulator arrived. 1 December 1975 was the first formal day of No 14 Squadron as a single-seat strike squadron. In March 1976 the Squadron first stood QRA.

NATO exercises, Lone Rangers (but seldom further than to Gibraltar or Italy), Decimomannu detachments, bird-strike speed restrictions, combined to continue the routine. One novelty was the premature curtailment of night flying one evening in August 1976 - the local residents got fed up with the noise and attempted to set fire to the runway approach lights. In early 1977 the Squadron gained a clean sweep of firsts in TACEVAL, and won the Salmond Trophy for the third time in succession. The stress was always on devising more realistic training by extending and complicating the equivalent strike sorties flown at the end of generation exercises.

By June 1978 the hardened accommodation was in full use: a trial was carried out of strike loading two aircraft in one Hardened Aircraft Shelter (HAS), and carrying out full authorisation and release procedures in the side-by-side posture. The Squadron strength at this time averaged 15 single-seaters plus 2 two-seaters for its, on average, 21 or 22 pilots. Good summer weather in 1978 meant often over 500 hours per month. In January 1979 there were, however, less than 250 to share around - the worst winter for 15 years. But all 21 pilots were classified as strike combat ready: rapid turnover in the preceding year or so meant that this 100% state was the first time in 19 months. Such skills had to be put to use and so in June 1979 a Wildenrath challenge to Brüggen was accepted and the result was the running of Exercise Strangle Sonata, aim: to destroy a piano on Nordhorn Range with practice bombs. Mission accomplished. August saw the Squadron engaged on a three-day intensive flying trial: 50 missions a day, many involving a full Operational Turn-Round, re-arming with 4x1000lb bombs and 2 gun-loads of 120x30mm rounds. 1001b bombs were released at the new cleared speed of 550 knots. The principal finding was that the really urgent need was for better HAS and filtered domestic accommodation. Not much intensive flying the next month: at the end of the month an indefinite 25% reduction in flying task was imposed as a result of UK industrial action affecting spares delivery. Things come back to normal for a November exchange with the F-104s at Gioia del Colle, good introduction, no doubt, to the Red Flag work-up which followed December's TACEVAL and found the Squadron in Nevada in February 1980. This saw the first 1001b Paveway laser-guided bomb (LBG) drop. The coordinated LGB attack, with designation provided by Buccaneers was first practised in August 1982, with some intensive live training, based at Lossiemouth the next month. The late-1982 MAXEVAL and MINEVAL tests both continued to mix strike and conventional weapon handling and flying profiles. 1983 sees the introduction of active ECM equipment, and first realistic use of it at February's Red Flag. 1984, still further operational enhancements with a visit from RAE to introduce Night Vision Goggles and Forward Looking Infra-Red methods and equipment.

By July 1984 the first RAF Germany Jaguar squadron is handing over to Tornado; that changeover then accelerated and when No 17 Squadron handed over in March 1985, 14 was the last fully operational single-seat strike unit in Germany. In May, Wing Commander Joe Whitfield led in the advance party and by 17 May the first Tornado was airborne on an acceptance check sortie. In August, by then with 22 Tornado aircrew, that half of the Squadron was working on practice weapon loading, weapon acceptance, release and launch procedures. In October 1985 the Tornado wing assumed the QRA task, and on 1 November 14 was officially declared as a Tornado Squadron. October 1986 marked the second visit of the Weapon Standardisation Team, and as the Form 540 said "The climax of the visit saw the Squadron demonstrate under full NBC conditions their ability to convoy a special weapon and deal expeditiously with an intruder incident." Here endeth the lesson, so to speak, since in a brief note at the end of that same Form 540 the Squadron Commander observes that "October also saw the end of QRA(N) at Brüggen after many years of permanent standby." The political and diplomatic process that led to that point must be left to another day. As a point in RAF Germany's history, it is certainly significant.

Not much to report since then, apart from the Gulf War. Also display flights at airfields in the Czech Republic, and at Schönefeld in former East Berlin, not necessarily unfamiliar to the target studies of 30 years before. But the nuclear capability remained, and was kept at appropriate levels of familiarity and competence, until that final moment this year when - as I said in the opening paragraph - the WE177 was withdrawn from service and the strike role was no longer a Royal Air Force function.

9. Offensive Operations - Attack

Air Commodore M G F White OBE

In 1974 Air Cdre Malcolm White began a long association with RAF Germany and the Harrier, which he flew with 3 Sqn at Wildenrath and 1 Sqn at Gütersloh. He returned to HQ RAF Germany in 1987, before becoming PSO to CAS in the early 1990s, then back to Germany again to command Laarbruch. He is currently Assistant Commandant (Air) at the Joint Services Command and Staff College.

While a chronological canter across attack operations from 1945 to date had its attractions, I have decided to concentrate on four areas; namely, doctrine, command and control, aircraft and basing, and training.

For my start date I have selected 1967 the year in which NATO adopted MC 14/3 and the strategy of flexible response, and with it a much greater emphasis on conventional attack operations. So, let me turn now to some of the issues which I believe have influenced our attack operations in the Central Region and first - doctrine.

Doctrine

Before the advent of MC 14/3 conventional attack operations were largely overshadowed by the nuclear umbrella. Following the Lisbon summit of 1952, MC 14/1 had assumed that if the Warsaw Pact invaded, a NATO screen would hold the line until US forces were in place to deliver an atomic response, following which NATO ground forces would recover what had been lost. By 1957 NATO had concluded that a follow-on 'mop-up operation' would not be required as there would be nothing left worth recovering. In short, NATO had come to rely on a nuclear capability to address the numerical inferiority of its conventional forces. At this stage offensive air was focused primarily on the interdiction of Warsaw Pact land forces based in East Germany, with Close Air Support (CAS) taking a secondary role, either to counter any breakthrough or to support allied land forces in the event of a late or incomplete mobilisation. Offensive Counter Air (OCA) appears to have been neglected in favour of layered air defences which at the time were more in keeping with the Alliance's defensive strategy. This approach survived until the mid-60s.

Under flexible response, NATO now placed new emphasis on conventional forces designed to deter, even defeat an all-out attack. Air Interdiction (AI) and Offensive Air Support (OAS) remained the primary roles for offensive air as Defensive Counter Air (DCA), including NATO's hardening programme and the modernisation of its air defences, was preferred to OCA operations as a counter to the Warsaw Pact's offensive air power. In 1970, three years after MC 14/3, SACEUR directed that the Military Agency for Standardization should form a working party to "develop a tactical air doctrine that would provide a common understanding of the role of air power in allied operations, and a set of common procedures for successfully implementing air operations". This work seems to mark the recognition that not only did diverging national doctrines require harmonisation, but also that any future conflict would need to be fought on a joint basis. As is the case today, the development of agreed doctrine took time and it was nearly six years before Allied Tactical Pamphlet (ATP) -33 saw the light of day.

In the drafting process the first significant differences in opinion over the command and control of offensive air power surfaced between the US dominated 4th Allied Tactical Air Force (4ATAF) in the south and the RAF influenced 2ATAF in the north - a theme which I will return to later. Although ATP-33 devoted a section to each of the NATO air operations, OAS and OCA later received a more detailed treatment in ATPs 27 and 42, respectively. Again, differences emerged between the USAF and her NATO partners, chiefly over Air Interdiction (AI) and the conduct of air operations in support of the air/land battle. The fault line for these differences remained the 2/4ATAF boundary and the differences in opinion, particularly over Battlefield Air Interdiction (BAI), remain with us today. Such differences, and the divergence in views over command and control underlined the need for the creation in 1974 of Headquarters Allied Air Forces Central Region (HQAAFCE).

Command and Control

As we have heard, by 1967 Headquarters Royal Air Force Germany (HQ RAFG) was firmly ensconced alongside HQ 2ATAF at Rheindahlen. In addition, these two air headquarters shared the 2000 office building with Headquarters Northern Army Group (HQ NORTHAG) and Headquarters British Army of the Rhine (HQ BAOR). This was not an arrangement which was matched in the Central Army Group (CENTAG) region where air and land head-quarters remained separated until December 1980. Quite apart from differences in doctrine, this difference in command arrangements may also explain the different approach of the two ATAFs to the conduct of the air/land battle. In the south, a highly centralised approach to command and control contrasted with the decentralised control of some air operations in 2ATAF.

Nowhere was this more stark than in the context of air/land operations, specifically the division between CAS, BAI and AI. At the heart of the debate was the close relationship that existed between NORTHAG and 2ATAF and a particularly British concern that the highly centralised control of AI assets would put at risk the provision of air support to land forces, beyond the immediate range of CAS. The solution was BAI, a half-way house which was responsive to the land commander's requirements, but controlled at ATAF/Army Group level except, that is, within the 1st British Corps area where, by 1976, a unique arrangement existed which enabled the Corps' Air Support Operations Centre (ASOC) to task the Harrier Force direct, without having to work through the higher headquarters - the Allied Tactical Operations Centres (ATOCs). This arrangement produced one of the most responsive offensive air tasking systems in NATO, an arrangement which was unique to UK Forces, the envy of other allied land formations, but one, it must be said, which made some airmen nervous, including a number of our own Commanders-in-Chief!

This aside the advent of HQAAFCE provided a much needed theatre-wide approach to the command of air operations, with control vested in subordinate Air Command Operations Centres (ACOCs) such as Maastricht and ATOCs such as Kalkar. But HQAAFCE achieved far more than the simple streamlining of air command and control in the Central Region. A flurry of operational plans were soon to emerge from the Headquarters covering the spectrum of air operations and, importantly, a much needed region-wide air space control plan - Supplan -M- which had been prepared by the staffs of 2ATAF. For the first time the crews of our offensive aircraft felt they had a better than evens chance of surviving NATO's air defences on their way home.

Aircraft and Basing

And now to the hardware. A further reason for selecting 1967 as my start date was that this was the year in which it was decided to withdraw from Geilenkirchen and marked the start of a period of stability in the location of our air bases which lasted until the closure of Gütersloh and Wildenrath in 1993. From a zenith of over 15 bases we were now down to just 4 - the 3 'Clutch' airfields and Gütersloh - each of which was to provide a home for our offensive forces in the coming years. The year also marked the start of a further period of change in aircraft basing and a substantial change in the make up and capability of our offensive front line.

Looking back it is possible to conclude that our equipment programme was driven more by what was available than by what was required and I am struck by how many of the aircraft deployed by the RAF in Germany were in some cases not only unfit for the purpose, but were also employed in a manner not envisaged in their original design concept. Given the scale of change across the period including the various influences on the international stage, the cancellation of the TSR2 and the rapid developments in technology this is hardly surprising. In particular, changes in strategy, doctrine, the operational environment and budgetary pressures were each to have an impact on the make up of our offensive front line and basing philosophy.

With the closure of Geilenkirchen the Canberra B(I)8s of No 3 Squadron moved to Laarbruch, where they remained until their withdrawal in the early 70s after 15 years service in Germany. Originally deployed in the tactical nuclear role, the aircraft also provided an excellent long range conventional attack capability from the relative security of the 'Clutch' airfields. The Canberra was due to be replaced by the TSR2, but following its cancellation a gap in the programme opened until the arrival of 3 squadrons of Phantom FGR2s based at Brüggen and two squadrons of the maritime attack aircraft - the Buccaneer - based at Laarbruch. Both were formidable machines which in addition to their strike role, formed the backbone of our conventional attack capability until the arrival of the Jaguar and Tornado.

Meanwhile, a technology demonstrator called the Harrier was

looking for a role and by 1972 three squadrons were deployed at Wildenrath. This placed the aircraft at extreme range from its principal customer, 1 (BR) Corps and so in 1977, following the Lightning / Phantom change, the Force moved to Güterlsoh as two 18 aircraft squadrons - the number and size of the squadrons being determined by the availability of HAS accommodation rather than any desire for economy. This arrangement survived until 'Options for Change' when the squadrons were reduced to 12 aircraft, re-equipped with the much improved and more capable GR5/7 and re-deployed to Laarbruch. The lesson here for those who favour large squadrons is, beware the scope for an LTC slice without the political implications of the loss of a squadron number plate!

Back at Brüggen between 1975 and 77 it was the turn of the Jaguar to replace the Phantom which was required for air defence duties in the UK and to replace the Lightning in Germany. With the Phantom's departure we lost a mighty capability which was not to be matched until the arrival of the Tornado starting in 1984. This aircraft was to replace both the Jaguar and the Buccaneer. At last we had a true low-level, day/night and all weather aircraft which was both fit for purpose and enabled the RAF to make a major contribution to NATO's OCA campaign. And, as events have a shown, especially in the Gulf, a master of its trade.

The rest, as the saying goes, is history. Options, DCS and now the SDR have each claimed elements of RAFG's offensive front line and next year the Harriers return to the UK, to be followed in 2002 by the Tornado.

Training

First, and as much as we all love to hate it - TACEVAL. It is perhaps worth recording that it was the RAF in Germany which was responsible for the creation of this evil, subsequently adopted ACE wide, and which did so much to enhance our operational capability.

Secondly, no piece on attack operations would be complete without recording the contribution made by Decimomannu in enhancing the operational capability of our offensive forces. Our withdrawal from Deci is something which I believe we may still live to regret, particularly as we withdraw to the UK with the inevitable pressures on air and range space not to mention the lost opportunity to train with our NATO partners in the Eurofighter era.

And finally, low flying. The low flying system in Germany was crucial to our ability to train effectively and, until the improvements in the UK's low flying system in the 70s, was the best available in Europe. Low flying was also fundamental to our very concept of operations as, unlike our US colleagues to the south, we were ill equipped to take on the formidable WP defences without the protection afforded by low-level penetration. The 1000 - feet limit introduced in 1990 marked the end of our ability to train effectively in Germany and arguably, even allowing for what the Americans call op tempo, was at the heart of the substantial increase in the time our front line air and ground crews were deployed away from base in the early 90s.

The Legacy

In closing, I would like to reflect on the legacy of our time in Germany. First, I am struck, through personal experience, just how much the demands of life in Germany and 2ATAF focused not only our equipment programme, but also our training. I well remember returning to the UK in 1978 to find that my new squadron in Strike Command was well off the pace in terms of knowledge, organisation and training. I was followed by a dozen ex-RAFG pilots who felt the same and following a period of considerable mistrust, our experience and training were taken into account.

Secondly, with the introduction of the Tornado GR 1/4 and Harrier GR7 our equipment programme has finally caught up with the requirements of the Central Region. Two aircraft which were procured as weapons systems and which at last have brought much needed precision to our conventional attack capability.

Thirdly, I would highlight how the RAFG Harrier's off base experience has helped to inform the RAF's thinking, if not funding, in the post Cold War expeditionary era.

Fourthly, the division in approach which existed between 2 and 4 ATAF has largely been put to bed with our adoption of USAF operational doctrine so successful employed in the Gulf. In the process, however, I believe we may have jeopardised our ability to respond effectively to the requirements of the land component.

Fifthly, and on the down side, as we leave Germany I see the RAF's approach becoming somewhat introspective. We have been exempt from the rigours of the NATO TACEVAL scene for too long, we have withdrawn from Deci as a result of financial pressures and an unfortunate influence of our UK-based AD requirements and, in the immediate aftermath of NATO reorganisation, we have witnessed the Central Region's air and land HQs separate and the influence of air in the ARRC diminished to an all time low.

Finally, in preparing for today, I have been struck by the scale of change which has been a constant theme throughout the RAF's time in Germany. But I suggest it has been our ability to adapt which has been one of our greatest strengths and has enabled us to make a significant contribution to the conduct of NATO offensive air operations in the Central Region and, indeed, to the operational capability of today's RAF offensive front line which has benefited greatly from the 'Germany experience', an experience which I believe was at the heart of our strong showing in the '91 Gulf War.

10. Reconnaissance

Air Commodore G R Pitchfork MBE

Graham Pitchfork's first flying tour was as a navigator on 31 Sqn at Laarbruch, later he spent many years flying Buccaneers, including command of 208 Sqn. Although he had just one flying tour in Germany, he held several posts in direct support of air operations in the Command. His final appointment was at MOD as a Director of Intelligence where he maintained close links with RAF Germany and the NATO intelligence communities.

Reconnaissance is as old as warfare; it was the first role for military aircraft and since those earliest days it has always formed part of a balanced air force. RAF Germany, and its predecessors, was constituted a multi-role air force and, thus, reconnaissance has formed a significant part of the Command's operational capability throughout its existence.

Reconnaissance requirements can be divided into 'strategic' or 'tactical.' Strategic is generally defined as reconnaissance that is conducted to support the planning of military, economic or political strategy. Tactical reconnaissance on the other hand is used to support the needs of the military commanders in a theatre of war or the immediate area of confrontation. As we know, RAF Germany was a tactical air force, hence its reconnaissance squadrons were almost entirely geared to tactical reconnaissance and I shall concentrate on this aspect.

The tactical requirement was achieved by two basic methods of collection. There was photographic reconnaissance when the aircrew merely operated the cameras over the target and the intelligence was derived from the detailed analysis and interpretation of aerial photographs by the photographic interpreters; the PIS. Secondly, there was fighter reconnaissance where the information was gathered visually by the aircrew as they took photographs of the target. An in-flight-report was normally transmitted and this was amplified by a full mission report once the photographs had been interpreted by the experts and a fuller debrief of the aircrew's observations had been carried out. This 'misrep' had to be transmitted thirty minutes after the recce aircraft had landed.

Post-war Era

Our interest starts with VE Day in May 1945 when there were three Reconnaissance Wings in the orbit of the RAF's Second Tactical Air Force each consisting of three squadrons. Within a year, this major capability of nine dedicated squadrons had been reduced to just one squadron in the newly designated British Air Forces of Occupation. That single unit was No 2 Squadron which had formed thirty-five years earlier as a recce squadron, a role it still fulfills today. It remained in Germany for the next 46 years; indeed, a review of the squadron's history would virtually cover the history of reconnaissance in RAF Germany.

The squadron was based initially at Celle and was equipped with the Spitfire XIV and XIX PR variants which had given such outstanding service during the war. With just one specialist reconnaissance squadron in theatre, one Flight fulfilled the tactical requirements with fighter reconnaissance and the other Flight had a photo recce role. Much of the work of the latter was in support of damage assessment and the re-building of the German infrastructure. Some of this work was conducted by detachments to Gatow.

Introduction of the Jet

With political tension increasing following the Berlin crisis and the start of the Korean war, an expansion of the reconnaissance force was implemented. The cannon-armed Meteor FR 9 and the unarmed PR 10 aircraft replaced 2 Squadron's Spitfires by the middle of 1950. Within a year, No 541 Squadron arrived in theatre and it assumed the photographic role leaving 2 Squadron to concentrate on fighter recce. The Meteor PR 10s were employed in mapping Germany and Holland in the aftermath of the war. Flying at 40,000 feet, this was a demanding role for the single pilot whose navigation aids amounted to a VHF radio and a G4F compass. By the end of 1951, No 79 Squadron had formed with the Meteor FR9 based initially at Gütersloh thus completing RAF Germany's first recce Wing for seven years.

Attached to the Wing was No 4 Mobile Field Photographic

squadron that provided the essential support service of camera technicians and the photographers who processed the film before the photo interpreters started their analysis. Another crucial element of the Recce Wing was the establishment on all tactical squadrons of an Army Ground Liaison Officer. I should also mention the photographic interpreters of the RAFVR who carried out annual visits to the squadrons in order to remain current. This concept of support to the reconnaissance squadrons continued throughout the history of RAF Germany and it continues today.

Needless to say, cameras are an integral part of reconnaissance and the arrival of the Meteors created a need for a more capable low-level camera. The F24 camera used in the Spitfire had given sterling service since the 1930s but it was unable to cope with the increased speed of the jets at low-level. As a result, the Vinten F95 camera, with a 4 or 12 inch lens, was introduced for the low-level role. This was a smaller camera and so three could be carried in the nose of the Meteors. It also had the great advantage that the aircrew could adjust the exposure time of the camera depending on light conditions and to take account of the speed and height of the aircraft. In the main, the camera operated at 4 or 8 frames per second. This outstanding camera remains in service to this day.

Before the demise of the Meteor, No 2 Squadron had moved to Wahn where a third Flight was added, This was a Belgian Air Force unit flying the F84 Thunderjet and it demonstrated the integrated nature of the NATO command.

The Swift, Canberra and Hunter Era

By the mid-fifties the Meteor was no match for the increasingly capable Warsaw Pact fighters and the arrival of the Swift FR 5 and the Canberra PR 8 gave RAF Germany a much improved reconnaissance capability. The formation of four Canberra squadrons based on the 'Clutch' airfields gave the Command no less than six dedicated reconnaissance squadrons. Although one of the Canberra squadrons disbanded in the late fifties, the other five squadrons continued to exist for another twelve years, providing RAF Germany's strongest recce force in the post-war years.

The Swift had proved unsatisfactory as a day fighter and it was modified for the recce role and equipped both 2 and 79 Squadrons based at Geilenkirchen and Gütersloh respectively. The nomadic 2 Squadron moved to Jever two years later. Although short on range, the Swift equipped with three nose cameras gave good service before giving way in April 1961 to the Hunter FR 10, argued by many to be one of the best fighter recce aircraft of all time.

The arrival of the Canberra with its suite of high and low-level cameras, its two-man crew and its long range at low-level brought a new capability to RAF Germany's tactical recce force. In addition, the Canberra had a night capability using F97 cameras mounted in the rear fuselage. The bomber version of the Canberra had a large bomb bay but in the PR version an additional fuel tank replaced the front half and the rear half was made into a flare bay capable of carrying a crate that held 256 two-inch photo flashes. However, flying at 1,200 feet, and emitting a few million candle power every two seconds, made one feel somewhat vulnerable. Further disadvantages were the limitations of the navigation equipment and the need for the navigator to operate the cameras from the nose and the photo-flash controls from his seat in the rear of the cockpit. For difficult targets this led to the need for two navigators and with crews established for one only, maintaining a limited night capability was at the expense of the air-craft's considerable day capability. Nevertheless, all crews remained proficient.

By the early 1960s No 79 Squadron had transferred its number-plate to No 4 squadron and the Hunter Recce Wing returned to Gütersloh where it would remain. Its primary role was the classic fighter recce, or Army Co-op, role in support of the ground commanders. The Canberras were often used in a similar role but their long range gave them a capability to penetrate deep into Warsaw Pact territory and, during the first stages of a conflict, they would fly pre-planned 'line searches' seeking enemy lines of advance, any build up of enemy armour and enemy river crossings. At an early alert state in the transition to war, the Canberra squadrons would disperse four or five aircraft to bare bases taking an element of their mobile field photographic unit. Conditions at airstrips such as De Peel in Holland were very basic. Following the increased tension after the erection of the Berlin Wall, a number of Inner German border recce flights were flown using an oblique mounted F52 camera fitted with a 48 inch lens. I recall using the airfield at Celle where a flight of Javelins of No 5 Squadron provided us with a fighter escort during our photo runs up and down the border. This evoked a response on the other side of the Inner German Border but all passed off without incident.

As the Chairman mentioned in his introduction, a major feature of the NATO recce scene during the 1960s and 70s was competitions and the names Sassoon, Royal Flush and Big Click will evoke many memories and emotions amongst ex-recce personnel. There are undoubtedly as many opinions about the value of these competitions as there are aircrew who took part.

There is no doubt that there was some value in these competitions particularly for the photographers and the photo interpreters. The aircrew selected for the small squadron teams also gained some value but the majority of the squadron crews were not involved. Hence, the stronger crews became more proficient at the expense of the less experienced and less capable who suffered through a lack of flying. During the period when I was involved in the sixties, gamesmanship and a 'win at all costs' attitude were prevalent in some teams and this restricted the opportunities for friendly and professional get-togethers where a free exchange of knowledge and ideas would have been the real value. Thus, I believe the competitions tended to be divisive, damaging a squadron's overall capability and I share the Chairman's view that the disadvantages outweighed the value. TACEVALS and exercises involving the whole squadron provided a great deal more realistic training that led to operational benefits and efficiency. The Red Flag exercises of later years highlighted this dramatically.

The Hunter and Canberra squadrons were fundamentally a day recce force and the increasing capability of the Warsaw Pact air defences dictated the need for more sophisticated sensors and more capable aircraft. The early seventies saw the demise of these two outstanding aircraft and a major reduction in RAF Germany's reconnaissance assets. An element of the Harrier force assumed the Hunter Wing's fighter recce role and the three Canberra squadrons were replaced by 2 Squadron which re-equipped with the Phantom at Laarbruch.

New Sensors

The Phantom, and its successor the Jaguar, introduced a new era of capability. The F95 camera remained a key feature but the introduction of infra-red photography and sideways-looking radar allied to a sophisticated navigation capability gave RAF Germany a good all-weather recce capability. The Phantom was also heavily armed making it a potent recce aircraft that still serves some Air Forces over twenty years later. The aircraft carried a large pod weighing over

2,000 1bs on the centre-line and housing all the sensors. These sensors were capable of producing up to seven strands of imagery that had to be viewed simultaneously. This created a requirement to process and interpret a huge amount of imagery and this gave rise to the need for much larger ground support teams. The traditional Mobile Field Photographic Unit was replaced by a sophisticated Reconnaissance Intelligence Centre, the RIC, which was made up of no less than ten vehicles. The RIC was sub-divided into two Flights - the Processing Flight and the Photo Interpretation Flight.

The great increase in imagery to be interpreted following a single sortie placed an enormous demand on the ground photographers and the photo interpreters but they adapted and continued to produce mission reports thirty minutes after engines shut-down. No other Air Force in NATO ever achieved this outstanding performance.

After six years of service, the Phantom was replaced by the single-seat Jaguar that also carried the reconnaissance sensors in a pod. The advent of miniaturisation created a smaller pod and the drag penalty was significantly less than the Phantom giving the Jaguar a greater range and greater manoeuverability. However, the low-level recon-naissance role in poor weather placed great demands on the single pilot and 2 Squadron suffered some early losses. To increase the squadron's night capability night-vision goggles were introduced but it was the introduction at the end of 1988 of the Tornado that provided RAF Germany with a full night, all weather reconnaissance capability.

In addition to its significantly improved navigation equipment, the Tornado with its two-man crew offered a major increase in capability. The internally carried electronic sensors with a video recording capability replaced the traditional wet film photographic processing. Using a video facility in the cockpit, the navigator could carry out in-flight play back and editing of the imagery and this allowed him to file an accurate in-flight report that was voice down-linked to a ground station. Within two years, RAF Germany's Tornado recce force was given the unexpected opportunity during the Gulf War to display the unique capabilities of the recce system. The aircraft proved to be an outstanding success and No 2 Squadron, nicknamed the 'Scudbusters', proved that the reputation gained by the dedicated reconnaissance forces of the RAF over an eighty year period was as good as ever. Indeed, their success with the Coalition

Air Forces reinforced the crucial need to maintain a dedicated and highly capable tactical reconnaissance force. Within a year of their return from the Gulf, and following a series of defence cuts, No 2 Squadron finally left Germany to be re-deployed to England thus heralding the end of RAF Germany's dedicated reconnaissance force which had been in place for forty-six years. Although RAF Germany ceased to exist at this time, it would be remiss to conclude without mentioning the limited but very effective capability of the Harrier Force based at Laarbruch that has a significant reconnaissance capability as a secondary role to its primary attack options.

11. Special Operations - Intelligence
Group Captain M R Killick

The first half of Mike Killick's RAF career was concerned with flying, mainly Valiants and Canberras, ending as OC 98 Sqn 1972/74. Thereafter his subsequent posts were all intelligence related, including CIO at Rheindahlen until his own retirement in 1993.

My first intelligence was as Chf Intel at the 2ATAF Joint Operations Centre at Maastricht in December 1974. This brought me in contact with RAFG and its national intelligence staff, an organisation which I was to close down nearly twenty years later. In discussion with Sir Andrew Wilson, it was agreed that I would tell you something of my last three tours in the RAF, as Defence and Air Attaché in Warsaw, Deputy Chief of BRIXMIS and as the final CIO at HQ RAFG.

The most cost-effective way to gather intelligence in Poland was by touring, using Range Rovers and Land Rovers. Tours were planned as Air or Ground, with RAF tours concentrating on airfields, aircraft and all air-related equipment, while Army tours concentrated on their own service targets. The teams would sleep out under canvas in summertime , but during the winter we used small privately-run hotels (whose proprietors were less likely to report on us than the management of one of the larger state-run enterprises). Poland is a fairly large country and we nearly always travelled across it by road. With the aim of shaking off any followers, we would go 'off road' some way from target and head for pre-planned hides or OPs.

By 1988, confidence building measures between NATO and the Warsaw Pact had resulted in all major exercises being notified in advance and observers from the 'opposition' being invited to attend.

It was a strange feeling to be able, quite openly, to pick up a MODUK colonel at Warsaw Airport and drive him into central Poland to stay at a Polish Army Officers Hotel (roughly the equivalent of our Officers Mess). We would spend the next few days watching the event and photographing anything we wished (although there is no doubt that we were not shown everything).

One of the highlights of the year for Air Attaché's to Warsaw Pact states (and Yugoslavia) was an annual conference which was hosted by the CIO at RAFG. The Air Attaché's team from Moscow would join us in Warsaw and we would travel from there to Rheindahlen in convoy. With appropriate desk officers from the MOD's DIS in attendance, each Air Attaché would review the previous twelve month's activity in his area of interest with BRIXMIS covering the GDR.

I left Warsaw in October 1989 to return to the UK to brush up my French and German and to attend the Special Duties Course before being posted to Berlin as Dep Chf BRIXMIS. In November 1989, while I was still preparing for my new appointment, the Berlin Wall was breached, Quite astonishingly, both the East Germans and the Soviets declined to react.

BRIXMIS, the British Commander's-in-Chiefs Mission to the Commanders of the Soviet Forces in Germany, had originally been set up on 16th September 1946, following the signing of the Robertson-Malinin Agreement. The Soviets made similar bilateral arrangements with both the USA and France, although the British mission was always the largest. By the mid-1950s, BRIXMIS had evolved into a purely intelligence gathering organisation. A wide variety of tour vehicles was employed over the years but the most popular, reliable and effective was the Mercedes Gelandewagen - a 'G-Wagen'. For some forty years the unit had an average of three tours actually in the field within the GDR, 364 days-a-year. Although some 20% of the GDR was covered by Permanent Restricted Areas (PRA), which BRIXMIS was forbidden to enter, the Soviets had so many troops and weapons and so much military equipment assigned to the GSFG and 16 TAA that we were still able to score many intelligence successes.

Perhaps the most unlikely of BRIXMIS' photographic intelligence gatherers were the two Chipmunks based at Gatow. Officially restricted to flights within a 20 miles radius of the centre of the city, one could occasionally 'accidentally' stray outside this limit.

Although BRIXMIS' ground and air activities continued for a time after the Wall had come down, German unification eventually brought an end to field operations, the last tour returning to Berlin on 2nd October 1990. On 10th December, at a ceremony held at the Mission House in Potsdam and attended by the Dep Cdr RAF Germany, AVM Peter Harding, and the Commander of 16 TAA, Lt-Gen Tarasenko, BRIXMIS was formally closed down.

On 1st June 1991 I arrived at Rheindahlen to take up my final appointment as CIO. With the continued run down of the GSFG and 16 TAA, however, it was quite clear that I was actually going to spend most of the next two years running down my own staff. During the same period, two of our most valuable listening posts, No 26 SU in Berlin and No 54 SU at Celle, would also shut down.

The fall of the Berlin Wall had a disturbing effect on the troops serving with the rapidly dwindling GSFG and 16 TAA whose increasing frequent contact with Westerners was beginning to make them appreciate how traumatic their return home might prove to be. On a weekend visit to Berlin my wife and I came across posters advertising Open Days at Damgarten and Grossenhain in July and August. To drive, unchallenged, past the Guardroom of a Soviet air base in my UK-registered private car, and, having given a grinning Soviet airman 10 DMs, to be waved on to drive down the taxiway, was, to say the least, a novel experience. For my little party then to be allowed to photograph absolutely anything that took our fancy was simply amazing. Nevertheless, it enabled us to produce one or two final snippets of intelligence for the delectation of the C-in-C and the DIS.

12. First Afternoon Discussion

AVM John Price: I believe that there were Chipmunks in Berlin, at Gatow. I wonder if someone could tell us what they were doing, how effective they were and how it was cleared with the Berlin Air Safety Centre?

Phil Wilkinson: There were two aircraft at Gatow and they were there for two reasons. To maintain an air presence in Berlin, along with the French and the Americans, and for that matter the Russians, and to provide air movements of our own around the sector at all times. That meant anywhere in the sector - that 20 statute mile limit within which, the Intelligence experts told us, there was never less than 10% of the Soviet ORBAT to be seen. At some time or another, examples of something like 95% of everything the Soviets and Warsaw Pact had, passed through that 20 mile circle. A bit of an advantage, therefore, to have an aircraft that could fly over the top and, if necessary, have a chap with a camera on board. Suffice to say that at 800 ft or so, even with a box Brownie, you could see the most extraordinary things. BRIXMIS personnel who flew, or were flown in, the Chipmunk were able to provide the Intelligence staffs with a constant stream of high quality visual reports backed up by good photographic evidence. It was co-ordinated in exactly the same way as any other flight. One phoned the Centre and said I'm getting airborne in 10 minutes; this is my call sign, and they said, 'Thank you'.

Sir Andrew Wilson: Those Chipmunks flew around Berlin for 40 years and, I think I'm correct in saying, we never had an engine failure of any sort. Not true?! Someone's going to correct me. Please tell us.....

Gp Capt Hans Neubroch: I flew the Chipmunk between 1957 and 1960. On one occasion I had a partial engine failure, and I had to land at Templehof, but on the earlier point I would offer two incidents. One Wednesday afternoon we were told that a SAM2, with its associated radar, had been seen at Glau - which was just outside the 20 mile limit. We did our usual circuit of Berlin and just short of Glau we went down to 250 feet, went across the 20 mile limit, and took very detailed photographs of it, particularly, the radar. The following day we flew the photos down to show the C-in-C. He was so impressed that he sent us to Frankfurt to show the Americans. We were told that by the Monday those photographs had been seen by President Eisenhower. The other incident concerns the Wall, which went up shortly after I left Berlin. My successor took the very first detailed photographs of the Wall in the very early hours of the day it actually went up.

AM Sir Frederick Sowrey: Could someone tell us a little more about access down the corridors? I know that, originally, fighter aircraft went down; then it was limited to transports. We wanted to put the Red Arrows down to do an air show over Berlin in the early 1970s, and we were actually dissuaded, or perhaps even prohibited, from doing so on the advice of the Ambassador. What would your view have been as C-in-C had you been consulted about putting an unarmed training aircraft down, albeit in fairly large numbers? - you must have nine to make a Diamond Nine! Would that have been regarded as being provocative or were we in fact being inhibited from exercising our rights because of political or diplomatic expediency?

Sir Andrew Wilson: I think it's the sort of thing we, as military people, like to do - to be seen to exercise our rights - but I am absolutely sure that no C-in-C would have contemplated authorising such a flight without discussing it with the Ambassador in Bonn, and he with the Minister in Berlin. On balance, I can't imagine that any of them would have allowed it, because it would undoubtedly have been played back and read the wrong way. The fact is that it never happened. We were anxious to preserve our rights, and to exercise them, throughout this period but in the end we were severely constrained.

'Jeff' Jefford: I was at Gatow in 1974 when we tried to have, well we did have, that air display, but every time we proposed a quasi-combat aeroplane it was turned down. I understood it was the BASC that turned us down because the Soviets would not provide a safe clearance. We asked for the Gemini pair, but a Jet Provost was seen as a Strikemaster; we asked for a Hunter two-seater - 'No, it's a fighter' - and the Red Arrows were turned down because the Gnat was a fighter - in India. That was the sort of argument, so we couldn't have anything other than transport aircraft. (After note: Having consulted OC Ops at the time, Sqn Ldr Mike Neil, it seems that our requests were vetoed by the diplomats, rather than the BASC. Technically, we would have been within our rights to fly anything into

Berlin but it was anticipated that the Russians would almost certainly have responded with a 'safety not guaranteed'. So, not wishing to provoke an incident, at least not over something as trivial as an air display, and not wishing to be seen to back down, we probably never put the question to the BASC. The Americans appear to have followed exactly the same policy with respect to their Open Days at Tempelhof, as they too fielded only strictly non-combat types. 'J' J)

Sir Anthony Skingsley: A point about jointery, which was an undercurrent to much of what was said this afternoon. I think we are in danger of losing some of the benefits, particularly in offensive air operations, that came out of the 2ATAF/NORTHAG collocated Headquarters. Air Cdre White mentioned the way the Harriers were tasked - there was only one reason that it was the only organisation tasked that way - none of the other air forces in the Central Region would trust the army to do it - because they didn't have the sort of relationship that we had developed in Germany.

Equally, someone said that AAFCE produced the SUPPLAN MIKE - the airspace management plan. It wasn't produced by AAFCE. It was raised by 2ATAF/NORTHAG; signed off by both C-in-Cs and submitted to AAFCE who said, 'Please can we hang on to this until we can make it a Central Region plan?' I don't think there was any other organisation in the Central Region at the time that was capable of writing that plan - and it all came out of jointery. We gained a tremendous amount, which we are now in danger of losing. The Strategic Defence Review has a lot of initiatives for jointery and I hope they work - but I think there's a severe danger that we shall lose a lot from not having the same relationship with the army as existed in that headquarters in Germany.

Sir Andrew Wilson: I endorse everything you have said. The great thing about Rheindahlen was being collocated and my fellow C-in-Cs will remember that you could walk out of your own door, across a corridor and straight into C-in-C BAOR's office - and this happened, regularly, both ways, so that you had intimate access all the time at that level - and this was mirrored all the way down. Since the two C-in-Cs were talking on a day-to-day basis, other people were talking - throughout the ATAF and at all the other interfaces with NORTHAG.

I also agree that there is a danger now - 'jointery' is fine, but it's not on an equal basis when you are in a 'Joint' HQ - all with different

colours and different positions. Leaving Rheindahlen is going to
make it much more difficult for us, as an air force, to influence senior
army, and other, army thinking. Joint Staff Colleges are an excellent
idea - that's one way to do it. Jointery is the way ahead. I'm not
fighting that at all, but we don't have the interfaces that we had before
and I think history will show that they played a very important role in
the mutual understanding between the British Army and the Royal
Air Force. I would even go so far as to say that the NATO interface,
which went through similar doors in a different collocated headquarters, had even greater effect because we undoubtedly had a major
influence on the development of tactics and everything else. Now that
we're not there (at Rheindahlen), although we're still rubbing
shoulders in Bosnia and elsewhere, there isn't that same day-to-day
tasking, done from the same ATOCs, and I think that there will be
serious effects.

Air Cdre Malcolm White: The NATO dimension is the one which
bothers me the most and it's certainly what we saw when we went
over to watch HQ ARRC exercising - their lack of air awareness; their
inability to train regularly; the fact that it is now 10 years since we
had a one-star Commander Air at 1 (BR) Corps and that its staff now
has no air representation above wing commander. All of this lead to
the problems that we had in Bosnia. As we look now, all I see is
separate 'air' and 'ground' in a NATO context - and HQ ARRC is
really the only show in town in the Central Region today. At home, I
think we've gone the other way. We've almost gone joint-mad. We've
got the permanent JHQ, which I think is a little bit too introspective,
although it works very well. You've got the JTF HQ, that goes out to
wherever the conflict is - and again, the structures are in place and the
training's in place. We've got this place and I think we'll find that,
living in this College, each service will understand what the others
can do far better than has been case, ever - certainly for the time I've
been in the Services.

Finally, there is this business of supporting the land battle and
doing it flexibly and responsibly. CAS will be there, but what we now
see is the army - particularly the US Army - with weapon systems that
can go 200-300 kms deep. Because they can do that, they want
control of the ground space 300 km deep. As a result, we have
problems with weapons and airspace deconfliction, communications,
and command and control - and all that does is slow down what we

can do. The Americans have thrown out Battlefield Air Interdiction - you now have Close Air Support or Air Interdiction and Air Interdiction only takes place outside the army's area of influence. So, what we're doing really is taking the impact that air could bring to bear on the land battle and applying it 300 km away or amongst a lot of hassle. This is an airspace control problem and the lack of flexibility it is bringing to our operations is a real concern. I think there are three problems. First, the way that NATO land and ground forces are now operating. Secondly, the fact that we, as a nation, are getting a bit too introspective as we pull back - although I do think we've got a far better understanding of one another. Finally, we are going to damage air's contribution to the air-land battle unless we sort out this AI, CAS, BAI business - who controls what bit of ground and airspace? That is a question over which we - the Brits - are now diverging from the American position.

Stuart Peach: Doctrinal divergence is clearly alive and well and it is now becoming quite serious. Last week I represented the RAF at the Future Army Study Period at the end of which the Chief of the General Staff, General Sir Roger Wheeler, made it clear to his assembled crowd of 60-odd brigadiers that his main focus was the fracture between air and land, and the fact that, in his view, despite our having all these 'joint' labels, we'd actually gone backwards in real co-operation throughout the 1990s. General Sir Mike Jackson, COMARRC, had made the same observation to us about four weeks earlier. So, this is a serious issue. We do what we can at Bracknell, but do not underestimate the importance of drawing from the historical lessons of the last 40 years. We need, as we withdraw from Germany, to focus on this, otherwise the operational consequences could be very severe.

13. The Early Years in a Global Context

Dr Christina Goulter

Dr Christina Goulter is a Senior Lecturer at the Joint Services Command and Staff College and is head of Air Power Academic Studies. Prior to this, between 1994 and 1997, she was Associate Professor of Strategy at the US Naval War College. A noted authoress, she is currently writing a book on British strategy and economic warfare during WWII.

What I want to do is to set the formative years of the RAF in Germany in context, as there are parallels with today. There is a tendency to view particularly the early years of RAF Germany in isolation, without appreciating the wider influences which explain the ebb and flow of the RAF's fortunes in Germany.

Many defence analysts today look back on the Cold War almost with affection, and are heard to say "at least we knew where we were then". I think it is very important to distinguish between the early Cold War period (between the late 1940s and the early 1960s). This was the period of greatest uncertainty and fear over Soviet intentions, but Britain was also compelled at the time to address challenges to her national interests beyond the main strategic focus of Europe.

Although Britain was retreating from Empire, obligations to old colonies and the Commonwealth, as well as protecting long term trade interests and SLOCs meant engagement in a number of regions, most notably in Malaya and then Korea. Britain subscribed to the USA led containment of communism policy, which meant meeting threats wherever they arose. Closer to home, a little later, the Middle East was described as "the most critical theatre politically". The security of the Iranian oilfields, the Suez canal and basing in the theatre all became major issues.

Britain had to face these various calls on her defence establishment at a point when she was close to bankruptcy after World War II, and an added complication was the rapid advance of technology since the end of the war. Advancing technology affected all facets of British strategy. At the highest level, the advent of nuclear weapons meant British participation in a nuclear 'trip-wire' strategy in Europe, and then the development of jet technology beyond the pioneering efforts of Britain during the war meant that Britain was left behind for a time, and had to buy US aircraft. New technology and the associated new skills added to the cost of defence.

In short, a European focus with a simultaneous global commitment were undertaken in a climate of serious financial constraint. Britain had very difficult strategic decisions to make, and all these had a bearing on the size and shape of the RAF in Germany.

The transformation of the British Air Forces of Occupation into 2 Tactical Air Force in 1951, and thus an ongoing role for the RAF in Germany, was important for a number of reasons. It demonstrated that Britain was prepared to remain engaged on the Continent, and in so doing Britain could retain her role as a world power. Without that Continental commitment, Britain would have difficulty claiming world power status, because she was retreating from Empire and was close to economic ruination after World War II.

Signal sending of this type was extremely important in the early Cold War period when the Soviets embarked on a number of probing actions designed to test the West's resolve. This is the main reason why the West's response to the Berlin Blockade was so important. It demonstrated to the Soviets that any Soviet aggression would be met, and, further, that the US and Britain had the means and will to strike deep into Soviet territory if need be. The implication was, of course, that the Western Allies could deliver a nuclear device if the Soviets pushed too far.

The threat of nuclear retaliation in response to Soviet aggression in Europe was, in fact, the only card the Western Allies could play, as both the US and Britain had let their conventional forces run down since the end of World War II. Within a year of war's end, US and British forces were one-quarter of their wartime strength. By 1947, the British Air Forces of Occupation comprised only ten squadrons, as compared with 1945's figure of thirty-six squadrons. Meanwhile, the Soviet forces maintained their wartime strength of over 4.5 million men. If the Soviet forces had launched a massive attack on the

Western Allies, it was very apparent that the West's conventional forces would, at best, only delay a Soviet advance.

This explains the total reliance in the early years of the Cold War in Europe on a nuclear deterrent. The RAF and other British forces based in Germany became part of the 'trip-wire' strategy, whereby any Soviet aggression would be met by a nuclear response. This strategy remained largely unmodified until 1951.

When NATO was created in 1949, in response largely to two acts of Soviet aggression in 1948 (the attack on Czechoslovakia and the Berlin Blockade) and the Soviet development of a atomic weapon, it was agreed that while most western European nations would place their air forces directly under the control of the Supreme Allied Commander Europe, the US and Britain would only 'assign' their air forces to NATO support in time of emergency, as it was recognised that these nations had global commitments.

Britain's global commitments did affect the size and nature of the RAF's establishment in Germany. In 1948, at the same time as the attack on Czechoslovakia and the Berlin Blockade, the Malayan Emergency began. Between 1948 and 1960, an average of ten RAF squadrons were involved in Malaya, and the operations carried out covered the range of capabilities which would be required in Europe in the event of war, everything from air defence, air support to transport roles.

Because of the involvement in Malaya, the RAF was unable to contribute to the extent desired in the Korean War, which began in June 1950. Three Sunderland squadrons were offered as the RAF's contribution. However, the Korean War had an important impact on the European theatre in some unexpected ways. Firstly, the combats between the USAF Sabres and the MiG-15s demonstrated that the RAF's own Meteor would be outclassed should it come into contact with MiGs in Europe, and, therefore, a hurried order for some 400 Sabres was placed with the US. Second, we must remember that this was still the period when Communism was seen as a monolithic block, controlled by Moscow, and there was a not unreasonable concern that the Communists' action in Korea was a feint to cover a major attack in the West. In the event, the weight of attack would fall on the RAF in Germany until the USAF could redeploy to Europe.

The deficiency of conventional forces in Europe led to the decision in 1951 to expand these forces. Eisenhower, as Supreme

Allied Commander Europe, was anxious to 'raise the nuclear threshold' in view of Soviet atomic capability. In response, the RAF's 2nd TAF was rapidly expanded, from 16 squadrons in 1951 to 25 in 1952, and 35 by 1955 (its peak strength).

In 1956, Britain was reminded again of her global interests when the Suez Crises came to a head. In response to Egypt's threat to nationalise the Suez Canal, Britain and France concentrated forces in Malta and Cyprus. Coming on top of Malaya and Korea, the Soviet support to the Egyptians confirmed for Britain that she would have to face Soviet probings throughout the world, and not only in Europe. It was clear that the West's response to such wars by proxy had to be conventional, at least to begin with, and this reinforced the line of development begun by Eisenhower's wish to raise the nuclear threshold. The resulting more flexible strategic concept which ultimately emerged is now referred to as 'flexible response'. This strategy demanding a balanced force structure, with a mix of conventional, tactical nuclear and strategic nuclear weapons. The danger of massive nuclear retaliation was, thus, significantly reduced.

However, the switch to this approach caused considerable alarm among defence budget drafters. It was realised that if NATO was to contain Warsaw Pact forces initially using conventional means, then an even greater expansion of conventional forces would be required. The problem was one of cost. The expansion of 2TAF had been less rapid than envisaged because simultaneously Britain was trying to build up her own strategic nuclear deterrent, and the cost of this had to be balanced by a reduced conventional outlay in the RAF's assets in Germany. The V-Force of Bomber Command became operational in mid-1955, and reached a peak strength in 1961 of 164 bombers in 17 squadrons. The creation of this force was the single most costly activity of the RAF up to 1969, but even in the mid-1950s, it was acknowledged that the RAF could not sustain the expansion of both conventional and nuclear forces. Therefore, after 1955, moves were made to reduce 2TAF, and the number of squadrons fell from 35 in 1955 to 33 a year later.

However, worse was to come for the RAF in Germany. The Sandys defence review of April 1957 called for a halving of 2TAF by March 1958 (Over 400 aircraft down to 216). Needless to say, this was not a popular announcement in any quarter, but the European allies were greatly alarmed. The greatest relative reduction was in fighter strength, and no answers were given as to how the British responsibility for air control of the eastern frontier would be fulfilled without interceptor fighters. Under Sandys, air defence across all of the RAF's overseas commitments (including Germany) was to be met by just six squadrons. There was also concern in some quarters, particularly as far as Eisenhower was concerned, over such a reduction at a time when the Germans were expanding their air force. Britain was asked by her Western European Union partners to have Canberra and fighter squadrons based in Britain detached to 2TAF under a rotation scheme. The deployment of Canberras in this way posed few problems, as the Canberras of Bomber Command were viewed primarily as a force in support of SACEUR. However, the rotation of UK based fighters was more difficult, as CAS (Sir Dermot Boyle) would not agree to even short term reductions in the Air Defence of the United Kingdom (ADUK) force, which was due to be radically reduced in size.

The Sandys approach of putting all the defensive eggs into the missile basket was all the more alarming in light of intelligence assessments of Soviet capability generally. A new Soviet strategic bomber was expected to come into service by 1960 or 1961, and improved light bombers were also anticipated. There were already some 275 Badger medium bombers in existence. Yet Sandys continued to argue that the more the West invested in conventional forces, the greater the damage to the nuclear deterrent, as it showed Britain and the US were prepared to fight a large scale conventional war. The launching of "Sputnik" in October 1957 reinforced for most people the idea that the Soviets were forging ahead in all technical areas.

Fortunately for the RAF, many of the decisions taken by Sandys were reversed after it became apparent that the various missile plans were either too costly or too inflexible for Britain's defence needs, but the budgetary pressure which began before the Sandys review continued, so that by 1962, RAF Germany (as 2TAF had become) had been reduced down to 12 squadrons, and this level remained constant for the next eight years. During the same period, most of Britain's overseas commitments remained largely intact, including responsibilities in the Middle East, and towards SEATO and ANZAM. As important as these commitments were, they were maintained largely at the expense of RAF Germany and ADUK.

Briefly, to conclude, RAF Germany and, thus, a Continental engagement, reinforced Britain's claim to be a world power, and this is as important today as it was back in the early Cold War period. To remain engaged on the Continent is prudent, even if Britain's commitment to Europe today is less pressing than during the Cold War. Whenever Britain has disengaged from the Continent, there have been problems, and this was seen most graphically last century but also during the 1930s. Signal sending in an age of uncertainty is still very important, especially when there is much jostling among states emerging from the Communist umbrella, and as Russia re-established her identity. As the Berlin airlift showed, power projection does not necessarily involve a shooting contest, only an implied shooting contest. As in the early Cold War, we are also in a position of having simultaneous global commitments. As the uncertainties over the international scene are even greater now, the wisdom of having a balanced force structure is clear. There was a tendency to argue just after the end of the Cold War that because certain roles were prominent during the Cold War these should be downplayed. Anti-submarine capability was one of those areas. The Sandys years showed the folly of cutting whole capabilities and forces in what will always remain a strategic focus for Britain: Europe. A presence in Germany has proved vital in recent operations in the Balkans, and all that is associated with operating forces outside of the UK makes British forces better equipped to deal with overseas deployment. Indeed, as other presenters have shown, the development of many procedures in RAF Germany was to benefit the RAF as a whole. The TACEVAL is a good example. Thus, it is possible to say that RAF Germany has been central to the RAF's existence since the early Cold War, even though it has not always had the emphasis it warranted.

14. Historical Perspective

Sebastian Cox

Sebastian Cox joined the Air Historical Branch of the MOD in 1984, and became Head of the Branch in 1996. He has written widely on the RAF and air power, and has lectured to military and civilian audiences in the UK, US, Canada, France, Germany, and New Zealand. As Head of AHB he is responsible for historical policy and writing for the RAF, and is currently leading the team researching and writing the history of the RAF in Operation GRANBY. He is also the editor of the successful book series Studies in Air Power published by Frank Cass.

I should like to discuss some of the wider political and military implications of what we have been hearing about today. I hope to show that the overall impact of RAF Germany and implicitly its sister organisation the British Army of the Rhine, was out of all proportion to the relative size and cost of the forces involved. Politically this was so from the very start of the period considered today. Not only did the RAF in Germany in the immediate post-war era demonstrate in the most practical manner the effective demolition of the Nazi military structure, but it went on to play a crucial role in the first, and very significant victory of the Cold War, namely the Berlin Airlift. The political consequences of that relatively bloodless triumph in the first serious test of strength with Soviet power in Europe are incalculable, but I would suggest to you the following as at least some of the consequences had the ball been dropped at that time. Firstly, the democratic politicians in West Berlin would have had little choice but to come to an accommodation with the Soviets had the West surrendered Berlin. The abandonment of German democrats in the city would have severely shaken the faith and resolution of the nascent democratic forces in Western Germany itself, and would correspondingly have heartened the communist parties not only in Germany, but also in France and Italy, which were both teetering on the edge of chaos. Had Germany as a whole either slipped directly under Communist control or been subject to a form of "Finlandisation", then the strengthening of Communist influence in France and Italy would almost certainly have prevented the formation of NATO. So, the non-aggressive use of US and British air power in Germany effectively preserved and nurtured German democracy and permitted the democratic development of Western Europe, leading ultimately to the establishment of both NATO and the EU. Without Operation PLAINFARE/VITTLES, we would have had no NATO, and without NATO the cohesion of the Western powers and constant engagement of the US would have been much more problematic, with Soviet influence correspondingly greatly enhanced.

Once the Cold War was firmly clamped in place with the Korean War, the RAF planned to expand its contribution to SACEUR's forces by increasing the size of RAF Germany three and a half times from 16 squadrons in 1951 to 56 by 1954. This plan was never to come to fruition. Essentially, it was undermined by Britain's poor economic performance - a factor that was to bedevil defence planning throughout the period, but which was particularly acute during the decades of the 1950s and 1960s. Such economic considerations were to be the main engines driving much of the policy, and the relative economy of nuclear weapons and a nuclear based strategy was the foundation of much of the thinking which influenced the size and shape of British forces, including RAF Germany. This philosophy was reinforced by a belief, stated bluntly in a Joint Intelligence Committee paper, that the Soviets were unlikely to move to all out war, but that they would seek to achieve their ends by political and economic means. The strengthening of the British economy by reducing the burden of defence expenditure was therefore very much a government objective.

RAF Germany was to become a target for successive attempts at reduction for much of the late 1950s and 1960s. For at least part of this period the Government and indeed, more surprisingly, the Air Council, would have been happy to see a far greater reduction in 2nd Tactical Air Force and RAF Germany than actually occurred. That the Government and the Air Council did not achieve their aim was due almost entirely to the workings of alliance politics. To put it bluntly, Ministers were afraid of the political reaction at home and abroad to any proposal to reduce defence commitments significantly, especially existing contributions to NATO. British attempts to change NATO's strategic posture were consistently aimed at producing an agreed alliance strategy that would make such reductions acceptable on apparently strategic grounds. Although alliance politics did not prevent swingeing reductions of 2nd TAF as the result of the Sandys review, from a peak of 36 squadrons, initially to 18, and ultimately to

12, it did preclude even more drastic cuts. We should therefore note that the political requirement to maintain air forces in RAF Germany actually helped to preserve and maintain elements of RAF strength and expertise which otherwise might have been lost. As Sir Roger Palin pointed out in his paper, the RAF and HMG planned to remove the air defence forces altogether from Germany. Part of the reason this did not in the event occur was the political sensitivities. For the Germans a force, which consisted solely of nuclear strike and associated recce aircraft, with no interceptor fighters, presented a double problem. Firstly, the political and PR problem of presenting this publicly, as well as the legal aspects of tripartite and quadripartite control, and the policing of the FRG's airspace. And secondly, and more fundamentally, because the reborn Luftwaffe was not yet ready to take on the role. I do not think it coincidental that RAF Germany was ultimately cut by 50 per cent only in 1990, when the threat was demonstrably much lessened.

By the early 1960s the first doubts over the strategy of massive retaliation had begun to appear. Although still accepting the essential primacy of the nuclear option the Chiefs of Staff argued in 1960 that the problem extended beyond the purely military and that the confidence of the allies and the continued belief on the part of the Soviets of alliance determination were vital factors. The CDS therefore concluded "we cannot admit, even to ourselves, that we would not fight on after a nuclear exchange, nor that we should not attempt to defend as much as possible of the territory of our continental allies." He argued that forces had to be equipped and trained with that in mind and that therefore to raise the possibility of reducing the role of conventional forces and their supporting structure within the alliance "might have disastrous consequences." This fear may have been exaggerated, but it would certainly have exposed differences between the British and Americans, who at the time formed the core of NATO, at a period when the Americans were increasingly favouring deliberately improving conventional forces in order to raise the nuclear threshold.

As the 1960s progressed the problems of the British economy worsened, and the costs of British forces overseas increased as the Balance of Payments problems and the fall in the value of Sterling hit home. The escalation of equipment costs did not help: the TSR2 would have cost 30 times more than the Canberra. In an attempt to solve such problems, as well as a desire to fund social spending, the Wilson government again turned its attention to cuts. It was again proposed to cut RAFG by fifty per cent. Some pious hopes were pinned to the prospect of arms control opening up such opportunities, but more realistic perhaps were the hopes of gaining an increase in the offset payments from the Federal Republic of Germany. One important factor in preserving the size of RAF Germany at the time was the attitude of France. As the Foreign Secretary pointed out in 1965, NATO cohesion had been badly shaken by the direction of French policy and Britain had to avoid any withdrawal of forces which had not been agreed with Allies in advance. The existence of secure second strike capabilities on both sides by the mid-1960s, and the increasing unreality of massive retaliation, eventually led to NATO adopting the strategy of flexible response in 1967, although the trend of thinking had been moving in that direction for several years. This did not stop Her Majesty's Government from attempting to withdraw from Germany to save on foreign exchange costs - the pretext being that increased warning time would allow their timely return in the event of crisis.

Let us move from these slightly depressing considerations to assessing some of the tangible, purely military, achievements of RAFG. Let us start with TACEVALs [Tactical Evaluations]. These started as a purely British initiative to assess the readiness and military capability of RAF units. The results so impressed NATO officers that the system was rapidly adopted by the alliance with inspections undertaken by NATO and not national teams. There can be no doubt that TACEVALs greatly increased the competence, professionalism and military readiness of the NATO air forces. They also contributed greatly to alliance cohesion and military flexibility, and to some degree of interoperability. Not the least of TACEVALs' achievements was to broaden understanding that flying skill alone was not enough. The penalty, of course, was a degree of social disruption and stress to those involved in them.

Having said that, there was also, as we have heard, an interesting divergence of doctrine between the British led 2ATAF and the US led 4ATAF. Whilst 2ATAF was firmly committed to operating at ultra low-level, the USAF, partly as a result of its Vietnam experience, but also under direction from General Bill Creech, had moved towards the approach we recognise today. This involved the putting together of large composite packages of aircraft moving into enemy territory under the protection of friendly fighters and with substantial support from SEAD [Suppression of Enemy Air Defences] aircraft such as EF111 Ravens and F4G Wild Weasels. It is impossible to say who was right, and whether one approach would have worked better in terms of attrition. Indeed, it may be that the existence of both operational doctrines operating simultaneously would itself have complicated and confused Soviet air operations. I do, however, have one serious doubt concerning the USAF/4ATAF approach, and that is simply whether it would have been possible in the face of a large scale Soviet conventional attack pressing forward into NATO territory to plan, put together and despatch the large composite packages in a timely and responsive fashion. One is nevertheless forced to admit that, to an extent, the RAF was making a virtue out of necessity, since the budget would not have borne the expense of the SEAD assets necessary had the Service adopted the USAF's methods. That said, as the official historian of the RAF, I would wish to associate myself with the earlier comments regarding the initial attacks during Operation GRANBY.

There is another question which stems from this and, of course, relates to assumptions implicit in NATO strategy and that is aircrew-to-aircraft ratios. Did we have too many aircraft and units with too few combat ready aircrews? If so, was it partly an attempt to put everything in the shop window in order to appear as strong as possible to bolster deterrence, or was it for domestic political reasons? One can make a strong case in favour of the former, and that ultimately, whatever the military weakness of the posture, politically it worked.

Which brings us on to intelligence, about which we have heard a certain amount this afternoon. Intelligence always has been, and always will be, a difficult art. There is little doubt that we exaggerated the threat, at least in terms of the capability of the Warsaw Pact forces and the quality of their training and equipment. To some extent at least, their forces were as hollow as ours were. In my view, and as we heard briefly this afternoon, there is strong case for suggesting that the Soviets too indulged in the art of the shop window, and that they would have had severe sustainability problems in some of their units had there been a war. Having said that it was always a central tenet of NATO thinking that western equipment was better than Soviet equipment, and that our people were better trained, and probably better motivated than theirs. Certainly some of the trials which were flown after German reunification exposed weaknesses both in Soviet aircraft, and the supporting doctrine and training. BUT, numbers have a persuasive power all of their own, and one could say precisely the same things about German or Soviet forces in 1941-1945, and we all know who won that one.

So to a degree exaggerated intelligence had the right result in maintaining a level of forces sufficient to deter and preserve democratic western Europe, where a significantly lower level of forces might have encountered a more adventurous Soviet foreign policy in Europe. Intelligence on the threat certainly provided an element of justification and philosophical underpinning for the expansion of NATO forces undertaken by Mrs Thatcher and Ronald Reagan, and indeed the 3 per cent of GDP increase agreed by all NATO nations at that time.

So to attempt a brief summing up - what did RAFG achieve and what lessons might be drawn? First politically. Starting with the Berlin Airlift, and the preservation of democracy, the contribution of British forces in Germany was absolutely crucial, I would suggest, to alliance cohesion and steadfastness. In the 1950s Britain provided the major political support for, but also a balancing influence on, the US core of NATO. Britain also provided a politically safe pair of European hands to own and deploy nuclear weapons. In the 1960s British forces provided the cement which filled the cracks opened by French policy under de Gaulle. Conversely, at a time when de Gaulle was still vetoing British entry into what was then the EEC it allowed a continuing and significant British political input to Europe. Britain, by her commitment to Germany, was also able to influence US policy to a far greater degree, and was better able to put the case for continuing large scale US involvement in Europe to counter the strong withdrawal lobby in the Senate led by such as Senator Symington. Had the British presence been reduced to the token suggested in some of the policy papers then the isolationist forces in the United States would have been greatly strengthened. Had that in turn led to a US withdrawal, or large scale reductions in US troop levels in Europe, then NATO would have been gravely weakened, and it is difficult to see how the Alliance would have found the unity and resolve to implement policies such as the successful Pershing/Cruise missile deployment in the 1980s.

In a more narrowly defined military sense RAFG's achievements were just as impressive. We have already pointed out the benefit of TACEVALs. I think there is little doubt that they were enormously beneficial both in honing the military skills of the RAF as a whole, and in ensuring that best practice from other Air Forces was taken on board at all levels of command. In addition the need to work very closely with the British Army and the physical proximity of the two services very much helped to ensure that the capability to conduct joint operations did not atrophy. I think it highly likely that the two services would have drifted apart to an unhealthy degree during the V-bomber era had it not been for the existence of the forces in Germany. The need to preserve a capability to support forces on the ground with both fire power and rotary and fixed wing air transport forces ensured that those capabilities survived, dangerously attenuated though they may have been at times. Had that expertise disappeared, and the RAF become a force almost solely devoted to nuclear strike and UK air defence, then I believe the success of more recent RAF operations in the Falklands and, especially, the Gulf would have been far more problematic. It is undoubtedly going to be a problem to preserve that degree of close co-operation at all levels of command when British forces withdraw from Germany in the near future.

In sum, therefore, I believe that the RAF forces in Germany have made a contribution to the overall military capability and development of the RAF and British forces as a whole out of all proportion to their relative size and cost. I also believe that their political contribution to the stability and survival of an independent and democratic Western Europe was vitally important throughout the Cold War, and probably proved crucial at two junctures, firstly in the immediate aftermath of World War II, and secondly at the time of the French withdrawal from the integrated NATO military structure.

14. Final Discussion

Gp Capt John O'Sullivan: Just a few words which pick up on what was said earlier on, and on what Dr Goulter was saying about TACEVAL. Despite its horrors, I've always been a great fan of TACEVAL and I think it played an important role - and not only in training people - it was a magnificent introduction to military deception, in that one desperately tried to conceal from the 'trappers' all that was going wrong on the station! It all produced an enormous sense of 'us and themism' and a determination which, I am sure, raised unit pride - I think it did a great deal for morale. It also demonstrated to our opponents that we were prepared, every month, to go through: the generation of aircraft; the defending of the station; the preparation to receive, what may have been instantaneous, probably chemical, attack; the launching of our own nuclear weapons and preparing to receive nuclear fall out. When I was at Brüggen, and I'm sure it was the same at all of the other RAFG stations, we never had an exercise without having our friends from East Germany and elsewhere all the way round the edge of the station with their cameras.

AVM John Herrington: Can I come back to the point about the Sandys' review and his desire to replace manned aeroplanes with missiles. We've heard today, and it has struck me in the past, that we have rather forgotten the importance of missiles, particularly longer range ones, in our co-ordinated air defence organisation. I wonder whether it was just a matter of cost that we didn't go into the missile business, or whether there was a psychological reaction after Sandys to say 'To hell with this - we won't have the missiles - we'll stick with manned aeroplanes.'

Sir Roger Palin: I would say, that the main drivers were cost and technology, and that the UK's air defence resources were focused primarily on the UK, rather than on the Continent. As I think I explained this morning, if you look at our island geography and the threat, it tends to drive you to fighters, because it is extraordinarily difficult to construct a comprehensive defence of the UK based on SAMs. I think it was natural that the Air Ministry, and then the Air Force Department, focused more on short range surface-to-air missiles rather than long range - particularly if you place that alongside what I also said about our presence in Germany which was, for political and financial reasons, more of a minimalist presence - what we could get away with, rather than going with the main stream on long range SAM development. So, my answer is that our position was not merely a reaction to Sandys, but a sensible, rational thought process.

Sebastian Cox: I believe that cost was the main factor - but it would be very difficult for an historian to pin down an influence as ill-defined as 'aggravation with the direction of previous policy' because it's not the sort of thing that people write down - or even put in their memoirs! Widening the question slightly, I would say that the UK has a problem in trying to keep up with too many technologies simultaneously. It was a problem in the Second World War and it is one that I think we've had ever since - simply in terms of the numbers of scientists and engineers that a country of this size can generate. So, it's not only that you have to compete with the Americans in terms of the amount of money they have to draw on. We have a problem, and it will continue to be a problem, especially now that there is pressure to divert much of our R&D and scientific base away from defence related industries.

Sir Andrew Wilson: Gareth Evans raised the question of a Patriot-type capability. I must say, having been in the Gulf myself, I wonder what history will say about our lack of a capability of that sort in the 'expeditionary' world in which we now find ourselves.

MRAF Sir Denis Spotswood: Would I not be right in saying that we did try with missiles - we had Blue Streak and Blue Steel - but none of them worked very well. So, I don't think that we discarded missiles entirely - but we weren't up to it.

Sir Anthony Skingsley: I would like to propose an addition to the list that Mr. Cox gave of the achievements of RAFG, because I consider that it was primarily responsible, not totally, but primarily responsible for the reputation that the RAF enjoys today, because, until about 5 years ago, it was the visible bit. It was about - what? - 15% of the air force, I suppose - but because of TACEVAL, and because it worked alongside the other air forces of the Central Region, month in, month out, it was visible and recognised. I would like to pay tribute here to the excellence of the men and women who worked in RAFG - and I am sure that none of the other C-in-Cs would quarrel with that. Two successive British Ambassadors in Bonn said to me, 'The strongest card in my hand is the quality of your Forces. When things are going badly with the Germans (as they sometimes did) the thing I can fall back on is the excellence of your contribution to the defence of the FRG.' My feeling is that this reputation, which I hope we still enjoy, was established by the people in Germany - not because they were any better than the people back home, but because they were on show.

Air Cdre Henry Probert: I remember a staff visit to Gütersloh in the mid-70s; I think we were opening a new school. The local mayor was present and while I was chatting to him we had had a lot of interruptions from Harriers. I asked the mayor what he felt about this - the noise and the disruption that it brought to the local town. He thought for a moment and said, 'We would much rather have your noise than Russian tanks.'

AVM Nigel Baldwin: I will take up a point made by Air Chief Marshal Skingsley, as to whether - and I'm not an RAF Germany man, I was with that other 85% (laughter) - there was a hollowness in that superb front that you all put up so well. Let me offer, as an analogy, BAOR. When the crunch came in the Gulf War, we worried about sending tanks to the desert. When we finally got them there, the armoured divisions were hollow indeed, because they had had to hollow out their resources back home in order to support one relatively small division in the desert. I wonder - was the Royal Air Force also hollow perhaps? I think a clue lies in its weapons. We've already talked about Tornados dive-bombing with 1,000 lbs bombs. So, how strong in depth was RAFG, especially in the less sexy areas - like weapons.

Sir Andrew Wilson: I think there's something in that, in the sense that throughout the 60s and 70s we were relying on 1,000 lbs bombs and BL755, which had some utility, but not a great deal. We didn't really meet this shortfall until we got some precision weapons - I mean JP233, a weapon designed to allow us to close Soviet airfields, and the Paveway series for stand off and low-level delivery. I think you are probably right, but I don't think we were alone. Only the Americans, I suggest, had the right suite of weapons - across the board - and for those who served in the ATOCs I think weapon planning was indeed a deficiency.

Malcolm White: I think we're still hollow - and we now have to await the arrival of things like Stormshadow, Brimstone, any extra buys of LGBs and so forth, which primarily come from the Gulf experience. In the 70s and 80s, before the 'T80 plus' generation of armour turned up, I think the CBU was adequate - and we didn't need a precision weapon in the Harrier at that stage, because we didn't have a precision aiming system. We were in the business of dropping 'football field size' weapons and, in the context of 3rd Shock Army and the 1 (BR) Corps area, the CBUs of the day were all right. We made a mistake by withdrawing SNEB, in my view - that was a very useful weapon. The Harriers didn't have access to 1,000 pounders and for the Jaguars we had to go out and buy things like CRV7 from the Canadians, because, quite simply, we didn't have the weapons to do the job. Right now - yes, we do have a precision capability, right across our offensive front line - but, we haven't got that much to deliver. Equally, one can argue that we shouldn't have to deliver as much, because we are going to hit what we want to hit whenever we want to. But until we get Stormshadow, Brimstone et al, and given the departure of JP233 from our inventory, I would say we are hollow on the weapons front.

Stuart Peach: I would like to widen the question slightly. As Sir Denis has reminded us, technology sometimes doesn't deliver, and we are tending to buy weapons that come in fancy containers which you do not open until 'the day'. They are very expensive, so we don't buy very many of them. As a result, we don't have the ability to train properly with them. When we look to the future, one of my concerns in the current debate over replacing Tornados with UAVs is - will we be able to train realistically with such weapons so that we will know that they are going to work? I think I am right in saying that we never really developed a proper way to test and train with JP233 - the test came in the desert in 1991. We are now buying increasingly sophisticated weapon systems which sit on the shelf and we hope that they are going to work on the day. Going back to AVM Robinson's question this morning - yes, we did, historically, fire missiles and guns and so on, but I wonder whether we will, in the future, be allowed to fire as many ALARMs and that sort of expensive weaponry as we would like to. Simulation may be an answer - but it's a big challenge for the future - will all this stuff work on the day?

Sebastian Cox: I have some sympathy with what Nigel Baldwin said. I would point out, however, that less than 10% of the weapons dropped in the Gulf were precision guided and that it is not true to say that non-precision guided munitions have no significant effect. There is now a tendency to believe that only a PGM is good enough. I don't think that is true - a lot of the unguided weapons dropped during the Gulf War did have a significant effect - even if it was only psychological.

Going back to the points made about the RAF's reputation - yes, to a degree, I think it was based on RAF Germany. There is an interesting parallel here with the French. Having withdrawn from NATO, when they joined in the Gulf War they found that they were not nearly as 'up to par' as they thought they were. We found some weaknesses in our own forces, of course, as did the Americans, but I think the French were rather surprised at how far behind the curve they were. One of the lessons that we might perhaps draw from today is the need to maintain our contacts with other air forces through the European Air Group. The more we can do in that direction, the better for the RAF - and for all of the other air forces, because many of the problems that we have been discussing come from being too insular - because you establish a mindset. Even TACEVAL produced a mindset - once you had generated the aircraft and launched your sorties, you had got your 'tick in the box'. TACEVAL never assessed real mission effectiveness - what happened when you dropped the weapon - because you didn't drop a live weapon, scored to see what it actually did to a T72. The more contact you have with other air forces the less likely you are to fall into the mindset trap.

Sir Roger Palin: Nigel's was a very good question, but it's a very difficult one on which to get a sense of perspective. Everybody has tended to agree that we were 'hollow in this and hollow in that'- but let's not forget the good bits! Our JP233 gave Schwarzkopf a unique capability - and look what was said about No 2 Sqn in connection with Scud-Busting - they were the only ones who could find them! Maybe I'm a bit defensive, because a lot of the combat crews in the Gulf came from RAFG, and I think they all performed magnificently. But there was one area where we were hollow and which hasn't been mentioned, although Sandy did refer to it earlier on - aircrew-aircraft ratios. As an air force, look what we had to do to produce enough crews - we had to lay on special training programmes and close the OCUs - the knock on effect after the Gulf War was enormous. That is a lesson that we mustn't forget.

Chairman's Closing Remarks

Air Chief Marshal Sir Andrew Wilson KCB AFC

The penultimate C-in-C having had the penultimate word, I'll have the last one by making just a few points. It seems to me quite incredible that of the Royal Air Force's 80-year history, 50 of them were spent in Germany but, as yet, we have had nothing serious written about it. I pay tribute to Air Marshal Lee, who produced a very interesting pamphlet which took us up to 1973, but it was a pamphlet, no more. Yet, as we have seen today, RAF Germany played an enormous part in the Alliance and in the overall history of the post-war period - and here we are with nothing written down. I hope that when today's proceedings are put into writing, what we have put on the table will provide something useful to be drawn on by future historians.

It only remains for me to say some thank you's on behalf of everyone. First, to those at Bracknell, and in the Graphics Office at Innsworth, who did all the hard work with the slides - there is always so much more than you see on the day. My particular thanks to Gp Capt Stuart Peach for his masterminding act, for his own presentation, and for his dedicated staff, particularly Sqn Ldr Peter Brown. I would also, through Air Cdre Malcolm White, thank the Commandant, Major General Granville-Chapman, for allowing us to hold this seminar here today. I'm sure that all of us who have enjoyed being at Bracknell in the past are delighted to be back here, to have been given access to the facilities of this marvellous room and to have had the current Advanced Staff Course here with us. We understand the situation in the future, but I know I speak on behalf of the Chairman of the Society when I say that we hope to have the privilege of coming back here - and to Watchfield - in the future.

Mainstay of BAFO in the early days,
a Tempest F II of 16 Squadron

Nine squadrons operated Venoms during the mid-50s,
these FBIs are from 98 Squadron based as Fassberg

15 of RAFG's squadrons operated Hunters,
mostly F4s like this one from 14 Squadron

An air defence stalwart, a Lightning F2A of 19 Squadron
based at Gütersloh

Betraying its naval origins a 15 Squadron Buccaneer,
successor to the Canberra in the strike/attack role

A 92 Squadron Phantom FGR2 firing its pod-mounted
20mm Vulcan cannon

RAFG's single-seat Jaguars were replaced in the strike-attack and reconnaissance roles by the two-seat Tornado. Photographed in 1984 when 31 Squadron changed-over-Tornado (nearest camera)

Royal Air Force Historical Society

The Royal Air Force has been in existence for over 80 years; the study of its history is deepening, and continues to be the subject of published works of consequence. Fresh attention is being given to the strategic assumptions under which military air power was first created and which largely determined policy and operations in both World Wars, the inter-war period, and in the era of Cold War tension. Material dealing with post-war history is now becoming available under the 30-year rule. These studies are important to academic historians and to the present and future members of the RAF.

The RAF Historical Society was formed in 1986 to provide a focus for interest in the history of the RAF. It does so by providing a setting for lectures and seminars in which those interested in the history of the RAF have the opportunity to meet those who participated in the evolution and implementation of policy. The Society believes that these events make an important contribution to the permanent record.

The Society normally holds three lectures or seminars a year in London, with occasional events in other parts of the country. Transcripts of lectures and seminars are published in the Journal of the RAF Historical Society, which is a publication free of charge to members. Individual membership is open to all with an interest in RAF history, whether or not they were in the Service. Although the Society has the approval of the Air Force Board, it is entirely self-financing.

Membership of the Society costs £15 per annum and further details may be obtained from the Membership Secretary, Dr Jack Dunham, Silverhill House, Coombe, Wotton-under-Edge, Gloucestershire. GL12 7ND (Tel : 01453-843362).